Praise for Michele Weiner Davis

'Michele Weiner Davis offers us major insights into how to solve the most devilish problem of marriage – loss of sexual desire. Her advice is uplifting and practical, and she never stoops to blame either the person who loses desire or the one no longer desired, since they are both victims'
George Weinberg, Ph.D., author of *Why Men Won't Commit*

'Michele Weiner Davis does a fantastic job of empathizing with and enlightening both partners in the sex-starved marriage. She highlights key issues and offers great tips for moving beyond the tragic stalemate in which so many partners find themselves'
Dr Laura Berman, co-author of *For Women Only: A Revolutionary Guide to Overcoming Sexual Dysfunction and Reclaiming Your Sex Life*

'I love this book. It is the antidote to the distance spouses feel when differences in sexual desire wreak havoc in their marriages. Discover the road back to true intimacy and connection'
Dr Gary Smalley, author of *Love Is a Decision*

'I am tremendously impressed with Weiner Davis's profound understanding of the sexual and relational quagmires so many couples fall into with their misconceptions. This book will definitely help readers to understand their own feelings, needs and responses. But even more importantly, it will help them understand the role of sexual intimacy in keeping marriages strong'
Dr Laura Schlessinger, author of *Ten Stupid Things Couples Do to Mess Up Their Relationships*

'Michele has done it again! For couples struggling with sexual problems, and most do so from time to time, this is the first book I will recommend!'
Howard J. Markman, Ph.D., co-author of *Fighting for Your Marriage*

A Couple's Guide

to Boosting Their

Marriage Libido

THE
SEX-STARVED
MARRIAGE

MICHELE
WEINER DAVIS

**SIMON &
SCHUSTER**

London · New York · Sydney · Toronto

A CBS COMPANY

First published in Great Britain by Simon & Schuster UK Ltd, 2004
A CBS COMPANY

5 7 9 10 8 6

Simon & Schuster UK Ltd
Africa House
64-78 Kingsway
London WC2B 6AH

www.simonsays.co.uk

Simon & Schuster Australia
Sydney

A CIP catalogue record for this book is available from the British Library

ISBN 10: 0-7432-5241-1
ISBN 13: 978-0-7432-5241-6

Printed and bound in the UK by
CPI Mackays, Chatham ME5 8TD

To Jim, my husband,
best friend, and lover.

After three decades
together, you are still the sexiest,
best-looking man around.

Contents

Foreword

Only someone with Michele Weiner Davis's expertise could write about the sexual drama that goes on behind the bedroom door with this much power. The decades she has spent helping couples are evident not just in the moving stories throughout this book, but also in the wisdom she shares on every page. You can tell from her down-to-earth, no-nonsense approach that she knows what she's talking about.

What's most impressive about this book is Michele's courage to tell it like it is. She doesn't mince words. Early in the book she tells us, "Fasten your seat belt," and she means it. She takes no prisoners, confronting men and women alike on the destructive patterns that destroy marriages. I've been researching sexuality and relationships for over twenty years and consider myself an expert in this area, but I was noticeably affected when I read parts that apply to me. I am a low-desire person, so I savored the parts of the book describing my experience; I found myself saying "Uh-huh. You go, girl!" Other times when her words made me squirm, I thought, "Hey, whose friend are you, Michele?" But knowing her as I do, I know above all that she's a friend of marriage. She's got the facts straight about what it takes to breathe life back into a relationship, and it includes men and women taking responsibility for what works.

There are countless parts of the book I'd like to celebrate, but I'll just whet your appetite with a couple of my favorites. Michele has the courage to say that if you're in a sex-starved marriage, even if no sex is not a problem for *you*, you *still* have a problem in your marriage. Far too many couples live with an unspoken, unworkable contract that goes something like this: "I expect you to be monogamous, but don't expect me to meet your sexual needs." You can't live under this contract without driving a stake into the heart of your marriage.

Another point I love is that knowing *why* you're not so interested in sex won't boost your desire one bit; *doing something about it will.* This is so true. In the past few years, we've spent a lot of time exploring childhood, studying human physiology, and looking at gender roles, all in the service of understanding why we are the way we are. Although sociologically important, this knowledge won't change anything unless you do something different. It's sad to say but I've seen many people use this understanding as an excuse *not* to change rather than an antidote to a sex-starved marriage.

I hope at some point you have the privilege of hearing Michele Weiner Davis in person. She's a powerhouse. I've heard her many times and always come away inspired; I'm pleased to say that this book inspired me in the same way as her lectures do. I'm delighted that her strength and inspiration come through loud and clear on the pages. At many points, I felt as though I were attending one of her live seminars yet getting her undivided attention at the same time. So taking her advice, I suggest you fasten your seat belt and enjoy the ride. This book is the way out of a sex-starved marriage.

PAT LOVE, Ed.D.
Author, *The Truth About Love*

Acknowledgments

Although this is my sixth book, writing is never easy for me. Take a talkative, enormously gregarious woman, place her in solitary confinement for months on end, and expect her to produce several hundred manuscript pages and emerge with her mental health intact. Thankfully, there are many people in my life whose assistance, information, friendship, and support make this daunting task a possibility. I thank them for that. They are my lifeline.

My family—my husband, Jim, daughter, Danielle, and son, Zachary—are especially appreciated for their patience and encouragement, especially when, during the past few months, I spent quality time with my computer instead of hanging out with them. When I completed my book, dusted myself off, and stepped out of solitary confinement, I emerged to find everyone healthy and happy. And despite my reclusive existence, it didn't go unnoticed that this was no coincidence: Jim was at the helm. Thank you, Jim, for doing all that you do for our family. And thank you too for the endless conversations about sex (the manuscript, of course) and your incisive feedback.

Many, many thanks to my other family—my mother, Elizabeth, father, Harry, and mother- and father-in-law Leah and Byll—for your support. Your love grounds me.

I especially thank Virginia Peeples, my dear friend and assistant. Besides skillfully handling every aspect of my business so that I can write unencumbered with any concern, you singlehandedly are undoubtedly the world's best cheering squad. Thank you for your undying belief in me and in the importance of the message I bring to couples. You are an integral part of this mission.

During the writing of this book, I have relied on many friends and colleagues for their ideas, feedback, information, or just plain old support, and they have given of themselves very generously. I truly appreciate this. In particular, I thank Diane Sollee, Shirley Glass, Azriela Jaffe, Jan Levine, Howard Markman, Betty Wilson, Arnold Woodruff, and Laura Yorke. I also want to thank Joe Peeples for sharing his wife, Virginia, with me.

I want Pat Love to know how much her excellent workshops, provocative writing, and endless willingness to share of herself have inspired me both professionally and personally. I expect they always will.

Sydny Miner deserves my appreciation for her encouragement and her adept editing ability, a skill to which I've now grown accustomed.

I thank Suzanne Gluck, who after so many years still believes in my work and my writing. Thanks for encouraging me to write this book for couples.

Finally, I owe a special gratitude to the many couples with whom I've worked and visitors to divorcebusting.com who have shared openly about the most sacred part of their relationships. I feel privileged to have been an intimate part of your lives and to have helped you to feel more connected to each other. I have learned a great deal from you. Thank you.

~ I ~

The Sex-Starved Marriage

~

CHAPTER ONE

The Sex-Starved Marriage

Dear Michele,

Please, please help me. I am going through hell!! I am twenty-eight years old, married with a three-year-old daughter. For the past three years, my wife has avoided being sexual with me. It has slowly gone from having sex maybe twice a week to now, if I'm lucky, once a month. And even then, it's not really having sex. It's more like her saying, "Hurry up and get in here, and let's do this before our child wakes up." There is no foreplay. She doesn't even kiss me. I'm the one who always is initiating any sort of affection.

I get completely angered, hurt, and resentful toward her because I can't understand how she could be so cruel to me. I want to tell her, "If you don't love me anymore, then we can split up and move on," but we have a child together, and I don't think that's right or fair to our daughter. I want to be there when my little girl wakes up in the morning and goes to bed at night. But I also don't want to be with a woman who doesn't want to be with me.

So I struggle every day with what I should do because I can't keep living like this. I'm miserable. I have talked to my wife about how I feel numerous times, and nothing I say seems to change anything. Is there anything else I can do besides getting a divorce? Is there something you could write to her so she hears from another person about the importance of a good sexual relationship in a marriage?

Does any of this sound familiar? Are these things you've thought or said to yourself? Or have you heard words like these uttered from your spouse in an attempt to get *you* to change? Either way, you need to know that you are not alone. It is estimated that one out of every three couples struggle with problems associated with low sexual desire. One study found that 20 percent of married couples have sex fewer than ten times a year! Complaints about low desire are the #1 problem brought to sex therapists.

And if you've been thinking that low sexual desire is only "a woman's thing," think again. Many sex experts believe that low sexual desire in men is America's best-kept secret. Just read what women have to say about what *really* goes on behind closed doors:

> I am so tired of reading articles in women's magazines and watching talk shows that perpetuate the myth that men are always more interested in sex than women. This is a bunch of hooey! There are many, many women who would LOVE to have a spouse who wants to have sex, touch, or kiss.
>
> I've spoken to many women who have this same problem. . . . Their husbands simply aren't interested. I cannot believe my circle of friends is so different from the average. None of their husbands are "getting it on the side" . . . they simply are not interested. In my case, my husband of 26 years has *never* been as interested as I in sex, and during the last 5 years our sex life has been nonexistent.

> This lack of sex is more than just a lack of physical attention. . . . It goes deep into a woman's heart. I think in a normal marriage, a couple can fight about anything, but then they can make love and soothe the bad feelings . . . sort of like a rebirth . . . a forgiving ritual. But when you are deprived of even that, bitterness and resentment and desperation accumulate. I have a husband who is a good guy, great father, good provider, but I have no lover. I'm angry about the wasted years, the years I could have been loving, but spent agonizing about why I was being deprived. It's so much more than sex. It's feeling wanted, and sexy and desired by the man that you are committed to for life.

As you can see, women have no corner on the low libido market. Maybe you're asking yourself, "If low sexual desire in men is commonplace, why are they so closed-mouthed about it?" That's a good question. When a woman lacks sexual desire, although it may be troubling to her, she's not likely to start questioning the core of her femininity. After all, she's almost supposed to have "headaches." Men, on the other hand, are thought to have only three things on their minds: sex, sex, and more sex. To be disinterested in sex is to feel less than a man. Just thinking about low libido, let alone talking about it, strikes terror in men because it threatens the very foundation on which their feelings of self-worth are based. No wonder they're tight-lipped. But make no mistake about it: there are millions of people, women *and* men, who just don't feel turned on.

It would be one thing if these lustless men and women were married to each other; they could agree to go off into the sunset, basking in platonic bliss. But as fate would have it, it rarely works that way. People with low sexual desire are generally married to partners who desperately yearn for more sexuality, intimacy, physical closeness, and connection. And this chasm between them—a desire discrepancy—spells trouble. How do I know?

I've been a marriage therapist for two decades. I've been privileged to hear the real stories of people's lives: the joys, the pain, the challenges, the payoffs. I've had a bird's-eye view of what truly happens to marriages in which one spouse has little or no desire for sex and the other yearns for it desperately. I can tell you without a shadow of a doubt that a marriage void of sexuality and intimacy is a marriage doomed to fail. Take Debra and Tom, for example.

When I met Debra and Tom, they had been married for ten years and had two sons, ages eight and five. They were strikingly handsome individuals, devoted parents, financially well off, in good health, and surrounded by loving and attentive friends and family. It's easy to understand why outsiders believed that they were the perfect couple. Yet despite all of this, their marriage was precipitously close to ending.

Debra spent much of our time together in counseling complaining about Tom. He was angry all the time and impatient with everyone in the family. His short-temper was poison to her soul. He snapped at her over the littlest things. He yelled at the kids "for just being kids." According to Debra, everyone always felt as if they were walking on eggshells. Debra also complained of Tom's lack of involvement at home. "He never seems to want to do anything as a couple or even as a family anymore. It's as if he's given up on our marriage," she said. "He never talks to me or even asks how my day was."

Tom had no shortage of negative things to report about their marriage either. He was quick to tell me that he didn't like being around Debra because all she ever did was complain. Whether he was completing a home improvement project or helping the kids with homework, Tom felt that Debra always found fault with him. Tom also talked about a deep disappointment in Debra as a companion. He wistfully recalled their early years of marriage: "She used to be fun to be with. She had a great sense of humor. She made me feel like I was the funniest man in the world. Now, everything is serious." And after a moment of silence he added, "We don't have anything in common anymore. She does her thing, and I do mine. At this point, I actually prefer it that way."

We met for several sessions, and very little changed. I was unable to help Debra and Tom find their way out of the exasperating labyrinth of blame versus counterblame. They were both more intent on being right than finding solutions to their long-standing problems. Nonetheless, Debra and Tom still claimed that they wanted to stay together. Yet I could see that unless something drastic changed, they were headed for marital disaster. Confused, I asked the couple, "What's the glue holding the two of you together?" and Tom's response offered the first real inkling of what had been really troubling them and why they had been so stuck.

Tom's tone softened considerably as he spoke. "I've given this a lot of thought, and besides staying together for the sake of our boys, I think I'm still holding out hope that some day we'll be able to recreate some of the feelings we had earlier in our marriage." And Tom proceeded to describe what he saw as the progressive unraveling of their intimate relationship.

Tom said that when they first married, he was passionately in love with Debra and found her irresistibly attractive. Their sex life was wonderful; they made love frequently, and he felt extremely close to her. His ability to satisfy Debra sexually made him feel good about himself as a lover and as her life partner. He recalled how their close sexual relationship reverberated throughout the rest of their marriage. They often snuggled on the couch while watching television, held hands when they walked, and kissed each other affectionately. He loved their time together. Tom felt that Debra was his best friend. All that changed after the birth of their first child.

Debra became extremely focused on her new role as mother, and when she wasn't caring for their baby, she felt fatigued. Sleep, not sex, was the only thing Debra found herself craving. Tom's need for companionship and intimacy was not one of Debra's top priorities. In fact, to hear Tom tell it, his needs were not a consideration for Debra at all.

Initially, he spoke to Debra about his hurt with this change in their lives. He told her that he didn't feel important anymore. He wondered why she wasn't into sex. He kept asking, "What's wrong? Did I do something wrong? Aren't you attracted to me anymore?" But because Debra was sleep deprived, hormonally altered, and overworked, she found herself having little compassion for her husband's feelings. In fact, she commented, "I couldn't believe he was complaining. I had so much to do with very little help from him. I felt like I had *two* babies, not one. It just seemed like he was jealous of our child, and I found that unfathomable. I never thought the man I married would be so selfish. After a day of taking care of our son's physical needs, the last thing I felt like doing was having one more person's needs to think about. I needed to think about me."

As the years passed, Debra's repeated rejections of her husband's advances hurt and angered Tom, and as a result, he stopped investing energy in their marriage. He focused on himself, his work, and his friends. And the more he distanced himself, the less inclined Debra felt to touch or kiss Tom, let alone have sex with him. "After all," she told herself, "why should I have sex when I don't feel close to him at all?" Now their infrequent sexual encounters, too often tainted by feelings of resentment and hurt, left them both feeling empty.

Finally their incessant blaming, their lack of empathy for each other's feelings, and their cold, inflexible body language that permeated our sessions made complete sense. Their marriage had become sex starved.

If you're asking yourself, "Now what does *that* mean?" I can see why. After all, the phrase, *sex starved* typically refers to a *person,* not a relationship. Sex-starved people are generally thought of in one of two ways: they're either so highly sexed that sexual satisfaction is a moving target, or they're people who, for a variety of reasons, haven't had sex in a such a long time that they're obsessed with it. But a sex-starved marriage is different.

Contrary to what you might be thinking, saying that a marriage is sex starved tells you virtually nothing about how much or how little sex a couple is actually having. It's not about numbers. It's not just about sexless couples who have slept in separate bedrooms for years. In fact, it includes couples who, according to national surveys, have an "average" amount of sex each month. Since, unlike vitamins, there are no recommended daily requirements to ensure a healthy sex life, a sex-starved marriage is more about the fallout that occurs when one spouse is deeply unhappy with his or her sexual relationship and this unhappiness is ignored, minimized, or dismissed. The resulting disintegration of the relationship encapsulates the real meaning of a sex-starved marriage.

Sex is an extremely important part of marriage. When it's good, it offers couples opportunities to give and receive physical pleasure, to connect emotionally and spiritually. It builds closeness, intimacy, and a sense of partnership. It defines their relationship as different from all others. Sex is a powerful tie that binds.

As with Debra and Tom, when one spouse isn't interested in sex, the touching, kissing, and other forms of physical affection and intimacy often cease as well. Spouses distance from each other emotionally. They carry on their lives together in much the same way that two toddlers might engage in parallel play—involved in similar activities in close proximity but without meaningful connection. Marriage becomes mechanical. Friendship often evaporates. Anger bubbles just below the surface. Misunderstandings abound. Emotional "divorce" becomes inevitable.

More highly sexed partners such as Tom feel confused and cheated by their spouses' lack of interest in their sex lives and try to figure out what's at the root of their partners' rejections. Unfortunately, they often assume the worst: "My wife isn't attracted to me," or "He must be having an affair," or "The kids' needs are more important than mine."

When people believe that their spouses aren't attracted to them, that their marriages or their feelings aren't important, or that an affair is brewing, they feel rejected, suspicious, hurt, resentful, and unloved. They start doubting themselves and their abilities to satisfy their spouses. They often feel deeply depressed about the void in their marriages.

When they try to explain these feelings to their partners, their explanations are often flatly dismissed. "You don't have the need to feel closer to me, you're just a sex maniac," or "If you would go to work in the *real* world rather than be home with the kids, you would understand why I'm so tired all the time," or "If you weren't so controlling, you would just accept that I'm not as physical as you are and you would leave me alone!" or "It's *only* sex. What's the big deal?"

However, to someone like Tom—the partner yearning for a better sexual relationship—being lovers *is* a big deal. It's much more than mere physical pleasure. It's connection, intimacy, closeness, and affection. It's about feeling attractive, feeling masculine or feminine, and feeling whole as a person. It's about being in love. It's about a feeling of oneness. But since people with low sexual desire aren't hungering for a sexual connection, they're not overly empathetic to their spouses' feelings and do little to make significant changes in their relationships.

Eventually, feelings of rejection become increasingly difficult to manage. Sadness turns to anger. Those yearning for more physical closeness vacillate between being distant and unpleasant. And although these behaviors are merely symptoms of underlying hurt, people with low sexual desire don't perceive their spouses' behavior quite so benevolently. Empathy is in short supply. Arguments about sex, or the lack of it, become the norm. Blame-slinging disagreements add to the already icy distance between spouses. Then, like a runaway train, it's not long before their bitterness and animosity collide head-on with every other aspect of their relationship. Nothing seems right anymore.

Does any of this sound familiar to you? Have you felt starved for a better sexual relationship with your spouse? Are you desperately yearning to be touched, held, fondled, and caressed? Have your pleas for closeness and more sexual connection fallen on deaf ears? Do you tell yourself that your spouse will never understand your sexual needs? Do you sometimes feel defeated—times when you've considered divorce or satisfying your needs for sexuality and intimacy outside your marriage?

Or on the other hand . . .

Are you someone whose sexual desire has plummeted out of sight? Do you feel mystified by your apparent disinterest in sex? Are you frustrated and angry about the never-ending arguments with your spouse? Have disappointment and hurt between you made intimacy an even less likely prospect? Or do you find yourself wishing that this whole "sex thing" would stop ruining your otherwise decent marriage?

If you answered yes to any of these questions, I implore you to keep reading because your marriage is at risk. Unsatisfying sexual relationships are the all-too-frequent causes of alienation, infidelity and divorce. Given our sobering divorce rate—one out of every two marriages dies—you cannot afford to be complaisant about the wedge between you and your spouse. You need to address this very important aspect of your relationship, and you need to do it now.

BUT I'M JUST NOT IN THE MOOD

If you have little or no appetite for sex, you might be thinking, "This is my spouse's problem. Why should I put energy into our sexual relationship if I don't really desire sex?" There are lots of good reasons. Let's talk turkey.

I've been a marriage therapist for a very long time, and I can tell you without hesitation that if you continue to look at the differences in your levels of sexual desire as your *spouse's* problem rather than as a *couple's* problem, you are courting disaster. Unless your spouse is superhuman with morals made of steel, s/he may not be willing to resist the temptation of having an extramarital affair. Late nights at the office with a seductive coworker, an attentive ear, and effusive ego-building compliments may be just the kindling your spouse needs to start a fiery sexual relationship with someone other than you. Infidelity is not something you want to experience. Having an unfaithful spouse is right up there on the short list of life's worst experiences. It's incredibly painful. Couples in my practice often tell me that healing from infidelity is one of the most challenging feats they've ever accomplished.

I tell you this not to scare you or make you feel threatened. I'm on your side. I want you to be fully informed about what your spouse might be feeling or thinking so that you can prevent unnecessary heartache. I also urge you to consider the unfairness of the tacit agreement you have had with your spouse so clearly pointed out in Dr. Pat Love's excellent book, *The Truth About Love.* It goes something like this: "I know you're sexually unhappy. Although I don't plan on doing anything about it, I still expect you to remain faithful." Can you see what's wrong with this picture?

Besides averting infidelity, there are other reasons you should consider making sexuality a more important aspect of your life. If you're like many people who are lukewarm toward or even turned off to sex, relationship issues might be a big part of what's standing in the way of your wanting to be close physically. For you, emotional disconnection to your spouse is a real libido buster.

If so, you need to know that once you start paying more attention to your sexual relationship, your spouse will become a happier person. And what does that have to do with feeling closer to your spouse emotionally? Everything. Happy people are more enjoyable to be around. They're nicer, more thoughtful, kinder, more loving, affectionate, and more communicative. It's a simple law of human nature. When you show your caring to your more highly sexed spouse by making sex a bigger priority in your marriage, s/he will appreciate your efforts and become more caring toward you. You will see it in his or her eyes. You'll start getting love notes and witness random acts of kindness. Your spouse will begin to open up and be decidedly more interested in you as a person. He'll stop what he's doing to hear about something you find interesting on television. She will notice your strengths rather than criticize. He will agree to go shopping with you to the mall. She'll give her blessings to that boys' night out for which you've been hankering. In short, a miracle will happen. It will take you back to the times in your relationship when everything was clicking.

Besides feeling closer to your spouse, there is another major perk to becoming more sexual, even if you aren't completely in the mood. You might discover something totally unexpected: your sexual appetite hasn't really vanished, it was merely camouflaged! Although I will explain this in greater detail in the next chapter, you need to know about some exciting new research. Until now, many experts in the field of human sexuality assumed that all people experience sexual desire in a similar way: something triggers a sexy thought, which triggers an urge to act—to become sexual with your partner or engage in self-pleasure. Sexual stimulation then makes you feel aroused.

But some experts are beginning to question this one-size-fits-all perspective on sexual desire. They've noticed that for some people, sexual desire—the urge to become sexual—doesn't *precede* feeling aroused; it actually follows it. In other words, some people rarely (or never) find themselves fantasizing about sex or feeling sexual urges, but when they're open to becoming sexual with their spouses anyway, they often find the sexual stimulation pleasurable, and they become aroused. Once aroused, there is a desire to continue. And that's every bit as much "sexual desire" as the more traditional view of things (Basson, 2001).

If as you're reading this you're thinking, "Yeah, that's me," you may be one of those people whose interest in sex doesn't kick in until you've been physically stimulated, and your body, rather than your mind, tells you it's time. Your desire to be sexual only happens once the right physical buttons have been pushed.

I am extremely excited by this new view of things because it describes to a tee what I've been observing in my practice for years. I wish I had a dollar for each time a person with little interest in sex has told me, "I really wasn't in the mood for sex at all because _____ [I had so much on my mind; I had things to do; it was too early in the morning; it was the wrong time of month], but once we got started, it was fun. I really enjoyed it." Eventually, rather than spend an inordinate amount of time analyzing the causes for the absence of sexual thoughts and fantasies, I started to experiment with coaching people to get their feet moving, even if their heads and hearts were someplace else.

At first, many were understandably cautious about my Nike-style approach to their sex life; the "Just Do It" advice ran counter to everything they had believed about how sexual desire unfolds. But I persisted, and I'm glad I did, because the results spoke for themselves. I could often see the relief on people's faces when they learned that their lack of out-of-the-blue sexual urges didn't necessarily signify a problem. It didn't mean there was something wrong with them or that something was missing from their marriages. It just meant that they experienced desire differently.

Second, when those who do not experience spontaneous lust really took to heart the idea that they weren't flawed, desireless, or sexually apathetic people, their self-concept shifted considerably. "After all," they told themselves, "once I get going, I guess I really get going." This allowed them to see themselves as more sexual, desirable, and sensual people, which, not surprisingly, often led to more frequent and satisfying sexual encounters.

But perhaps you're thinking, "Just do it? That sounds way too simple to me," or "Even if I get going, nothing happens," or "I just don't have orgasms anymore, and that's why sex holds no interest for me." Unfortunately, as you are about to learn in Chapter 2, feeling more sexual isn't always just a matter of getting your feet moving. Your reasons for feeling disinterested might be considerably more complicated than that. A healthy sex drive is dependent on a number of complex and often interacting factors. Many things—fluctuating hormones, medication (even birth control pills!), and illness—can greatly affect how you feel about being physical with your spouse. In Chapter 2, I identify the main contributing factors to low sexual desire to help you understand your feelings better.

Having said that, I want to caution you about something. Knowing why you're not so interested in sex won't boost your desire one bit. Doing something about it will. I know many people who become experts on why they've been avoiding physical contact with their spouses while their sex lives continue to go down the tubes. So though it's extremely important for you to identify the potential causes of your lack of desire, it's even more important that you commit to doing something with the information you uncover.

As unromantic as it might sound, even for your more highly sexed spouse, once the intense infatuation characteristic of early relationships wears off (and it always does), desire is really a decision. You have to *decide* to make having a vibrant, exciting, emotionally satisfying sexual relationship a priority. You have to continually discover and rediscover new ways to keep your sexual energy alive. You must consciously work at understanding and keeping up with the changes in your body, your marriage, and the day-to-day demands of your life so that you can keep on reinventing your intimate relationship when it grows stale. It doesn't just happen. You have to make it happen.

With that in mind, you should congratulate yourself right now. There are millions of people in your shoes who are too busy sweeping things under the carpet to acknowledge there's a problem, or simply don't care about their passionless marriages to be reading this book. Instead, they'd be focusing on their spouse's angry behavior and feeling justified for being abstinent for the rest of their lives. You're way ahead of the game. Good for you!

Perhaps you're ready to take your marriage to a better, more loving place. Perhaps you're starting to wonder whether your little inner voice—the one that whispers, "I'm just not a sexual person"—may be completely off base. Although you feel somewhat certain that you may never be someone who swings from chandeliers or thinks that sex is the most important thing in the world, you're starting to question whether a satisfying sex life is still within your reach. It is. You just have to believe it is and then take steps to make it happen. I will show you the way.

THE HIGH-DESIRE SPOUSE

If you're the person who's been hungering for a better sex life, I wouldn't be surprised if you're feeling relieved right now because up until you got your hands on this book, you've felt like the forgotten spouse. You've been frustrated by the fact that a great deal of the information available about low sexual desire is geared toward your spouse. And perhaps you've pondered the irony in the fact that the preponderance of help for low sexual desire is aimed at people who may not even see it as a problem. That's like writing books for people who are overweight or depressed but feel perfectly content with the way they are. What's the use in valuable information if the people who could benefit from it don't think they need it? That might explain why the piles of books or articles that you've given your spouse on the topic of low sexual desire have become nothing more than an impressive collection of dust collectors.

If your spouse hasn't been very receptive to the idea of improving your sex life, you probably have been feeling frustrated and powerless. You shudder at the thought that your spouse has been calling all the shots when it comes to lovemaking. But the truth is, more than anything else, you have been feeling rejected, hurt, and alone. And now, as you read this book, my guess is that you probably feel comforted that someone is putting your feelings into words.

However, just when you start to think, "See, I told you so! I'm right about our sex life," you shouldn't get smug. Do yourself a favor, and don't indulge in this sort of self-righteous reflection. Not only is it sorely short-sighted, it's just plain wrong. Even if your spouse's lack of interest in sex stems from personal or physiological causes, you're still not exempt from examining your role in your less-than-satisfying marriage.

As someone who specializes in working with couples, I can tell you that problems in marriage are almost always due to the ways in which *both* spouses handle challenging situations. When it comes to your sexual differences, if you have been feeling hurt or rejected, I can safely predict that your approach to your desire gap has been less than sterling. Feelings of hurt and rejection often lead to defensiveness, not collaborative solutions. You will need to examine what you've been thinking, feeling, doing, and saying that might be backfiring; pushing your spouse away rather than bringing him or her closer. You need to become a less reactive, more effective catalyst for positive relationship change. But how?

First of all, you need to understand the real causes of low sexual desire because your favorite theories about your spouse's behavior are probably destructive and inaccurate. For example, you might be thinking that your spouse has been withholding affection out of a lack of love for you. A person's sex drive may have little or nothing to do with his or her level of love for his or her spouse. In fact, your spouse may love you completely, with all her or his heart and soul, and yet still not desire sex. Or you might believe your spouse is avoiding intimacy out of mean-spiritedness or vindictiveness. Although a lack of interest in sex has varied causes, generally the intentional desire to impose pain isn't one of them. Your spouse isn't trying to hurt you on purpose. When you truly take this to heart, it will take the sting out of your reactions to him or her.

Once you stop recycling inaccurate theories about your spouse, you will become more clear-headed, enabling you to educate yourself with the concrete, reliable information about low sexual desire in this book. This will offer you greater understanding and empathy, which will allow you to more readily apply the proven passion-restoring techniques I will share with you.

Second, since I've been helping couples improve their marriages for years, I have a pretty good idea about which strategies work and which ones don't. And oddly enough, sometimes the most logical, straightforward approaches to relationship dilemmas simply don't work. That's why I want to offer you a brand new passion-building toolkit filled with ideas that have been field-tested so that you can make your marriage more loving and satisfying. I want to coach you to find better ways to achieve greater intimacy and connection with that most important person in your life.

DOING IT TOGETHER

Maybe you've noticed that until now, I've been talking to one spouse or the other, not both. That's because it is often the case that one spouse is more motivated than the other to read a self-help book or consciously participate in marriage-improving activities. If that's true in your marriage, don't despair. I've learned that marriages can change and grow tremendously even if only one spouse is actively working on things. You'll learn a great deal about this later, but relationships are such that if one person changes, the relationship must change. You just need one person who's willing to tip over the first domino.

But your marriage might be different. Maybe you and your spouse actually agree that your sex life needs some more pizzazz. In fact, maybe you've decided to read this book together. If so, that's great! (Why not buy two?) You'll learn a lot, and you'll be able to use what you learn as a launching point for constructive discussion. And that will be a good thing because it is too often the case that when couples experience sexual difficulties, they suffer in silence. They avoid talking about sex openly and honestly because it is too uncomfortable and embarrassing.

That's too bad, because most people are pretty lousy mind readers, especially when it comes to sexual fulfillment. We don't know what our partners need and want unless they teach us. Many serious problems with sexuality can be traced to poor or nonexistent communication skills around this sensitive subject. So I'm going to get you talking—talking and touching. *The Sex-Starved Marriage* will offer you specific guidelines for approaching the lull in your sex life as a team.

If you're the spouse whose libido has been lacking, you need to recognize that the most powerful sexual organ in the human body is the one between your ears; in order to feel more sexual, you first have to *decide* that a loving, satisfying sex life is important. Then you need to make a commitment to find your untapped sexuality within.

As the spouse with greater sexual energy, you need to approach your partner with greater understanding, compassion, and wisdom and learn skills that will lead to improved communication, compromise, and acceptance. And *The Sex-Starved Marriage*—the *couples'* manual for overcoming low sexual desire—will show you how to become loving allies in your search for solutions.

~II~

The Low-Desire Spouse's Guide for Boosting the Marriage Libido

~

CHAPTER TWO

The Lowdown on Low Sexual Desire

I n this chapter, I explain what low sexual desire is, what it isn't, and how to know when it's time to place more emphasis on your sexual relationship. Although I will be talking mostly to the spouse with less desire, if you're the more highly sexed spouse, read this chapter anyway because it will help you understand what's going on in your relationship.

First, you should know that everyone, even highly sexed people, experiences occasional hills and valleys in their sex drive. It doesn't mean they have low sexual desire. Sometimes a lack of interest in sex is a passing phase. You may have a lot on your mind, you may be feeling particularly stressed out, or you might be in a solitary mood. We all have those times. As long as your disinterest doesn't last beyond a few weeks, don't get bent out of shape about it. Take a deep breath and relax. You might feel more like yourself soon.

What if your feeling turned off isn't so temporary? Maybe your libido has vanished in thin air, and it's nowhere to be found. Perhaps sex used to be much more important to you, and you're wondering what's going on. Or maybe, the constant bickering with your spouse has gotten you questioning whether you really do have a problem.

Here are what some people have to say about their sexual desire.

When you're taking care of small children and cleaning house all day, your husband's needs begin to feel like another chore. It doesn't feel like it's for you, no matter how giving your partner is in bed. You just flat out don't want to be touched. It's so hard to go from being mom to relaxing and romance.

———————

My wife makes more money than I do, so we've agreed that her job comes first. She doesn't appreciate what I do to make our family run. I work around her schedule, I get our four kids off to school in the morning, I'm there when they get home, I do doctor appointments and parent-teacher conferences. But when my wife comes home, all she does is nag. Then she gets mad when I have no desire to kiss or hug her or even make love. I know our sex life stinks, but what can I say? I'm not into it.

———————

I work full time outside of the home, have a very active four-year-old son, manage a household, and have aging parents. My sex drive used to be in overdrive. I devoted many hours a week making plans and ensuring everything (candles, music) was just right. Now my sex drive is in reverse. Lately, our sex life has been nada!

———————

I'm a fifty-two-year-old man who has no idea what's happened to my sex drive. I used to think about sex at the drop of a hat. But now, I can go for days without thinking about it at all. I've always considered myself quite the ladies' man, but not anymore. None of my golf buddies talk about their sex lives, so I don't really know if there's something wrong with me or not.

Does any of this hit home? Perhaps your life circumstances are different—you have no children, you're in a second marriage and blending families, or maybe you're newly married—but do you still find yourself:

Going to bed earlier or later than your spouse just to avoid the possibility s/he might get amorous?

Lying in bed at night, careful not to stir for fear that s/he might start touching you?

Being sexual out of guilt rather than feeling desirous?

And if I haven't hit the mark just yet, have you ever said any of the following?

"By the end of the day, I'm just too tired for sex."

"If you had to work as hard as I do, maybe you'd understand why I have no interest in sex."

"How can we have sex? The kids are always around."

"If you were nicer to me, maybe I'd be interested."

"Why do you always have to touch me in a sexual way?"

"If you weren't such a sex fanatic, I'd probably want more sex."

"If you'd help more around the house, I'd want to be closer to you sexually."

"I just don't feel turned on anymore."

"I have a lot on my mind right now. Sex is just not all that important to me."

No, I haven't been camping out in your living room or bedroom. I've been counseling couples for years, and feelings such as these are common—very common in fact. Some studies suggest that as high as 50 percent of women and 20 percent of men say their sex drive isn't what it used to be. But what exactly is low sexual desire?

The American Psychiatric Association classifies low sexual desire in a reference book called *The Diagnostic and Statistical Manual of Mental Disorders.* If your lack of interest in sex or lack of sexual thoughts or fantasies is persistent or recurring and it distresses you or creates problems in your marriage, you would be diagnosed as experiencing hypoactive sexual desire disorder, or HSDD. The prefix *hypo* means "less than" or "under," as in "less than normal" or "underactive." Don't be put off by the term *disorder.* You are not a deviant. You are not sick or ill. There are undoubtedly many reasonable explanations for why you're feeling (or not feeling) what you're feeling about sex. In fact, there are many sex experts who, because low sexual desire is so common, oppose the use of the term *disorder* entirely. The important thing for you to remember is that feeling less than lusty doesn't mean there's something wrong with you as a person.

So, how do you know if you should actively be doing something to improve your sexual relationship? Let me spell this out for you as simply as I can. In my opinion, there are two conditions that should prompt you to take your sexual relationship off the back burner: when *you* think your sexual desire is a problem or when *your spouse* is unhappy sexually.

I'M WORRIED ABOUT MY SEXUAL DESIRE

If you've been unhappy about the drop in your sex drive, I don't need to convince you that it's important to do something about it. You already know that. I will help you understand your feelings better and then help you identify the steps you need to take to make your marriage more passionate again. Thanks to research in the field of human sexuality, people struggling with low sexual desire have many more options than they did in the past. There is no reason that anyone wanting a satisfying sexual relationship can't have one. Just keep in mind that the most important step in the change process is the *decision* to change. You've already taken this step.

If you're a woman, taking this step might be somewhat easier than if you're a man. That's because society half expects you to "have headaches." As a man, not being "in the mood" makes it harder for you to believe that you are not flawed as a person because you probably think you're the only guy in the world who feels the way you do. Let me remind you, you're not. Based on my clinical observations and conversations with colleagues, low sexual desire in men is considerably more rampant than many people think. When maleness is defined as sexual prowess or by the size of one's sexual appetite and penis, few men in their right minds want to tell the world that sex isn't very important to them. (And, by the way, although most people assume that the only reason a man might not be interested in sex is that he's experiencing other sexual problems such as impotence, it simply isn't true. Despite men's uneasiness about discussing it, there are countless men whose sexual machinery works fine, but they just don't feel like using it.)

If, on the other hand, you're confused about whether you have low sexual desire or if you should take your sexual relationship more seriously,

I'm not surprised. I say that because low sexual desire is a slippery concept. In a moment, you'll understand why.

HOW MUCH SEX IS ENOUGH SEX?

Most couples with a desire gap have disagreements about how much sex is enough. The person with less desire thinks that his or her spouse is oversexed. The person with more desire thinks just the reverse. Perhaps you've tried to settle matters, as couples in my practice have, by inquiring about the average number of times per week or month married people of various ages make love. Although these data exist, they're useless because what one person or couple finds satisfying is grounds for concern or divorce in another person or couple. Statistics don't tell you anything about *you* or *your marriage.*

Wendy, a woman in her mid-thirties, came to my office because she was very upset about her waning sex drive. Until her thirty-first birthday, she and her husband usually had sex four to five times a week. In recent years, however, Wendy estimated that they had sex two or three times a week. Although I reassured her that their level of sexual frequency was well within national averages, she was not consoled. Wendy had always thought of herself as a very sexual person. This drop in her sex drive, though not enormous, was enough to leave her questioning her self-concept and feeling unsettled.

Now compare Wendy's reaction to that of Brenda's. Shortly after I met Brenda and her husband, Bill, also in their early thirties, Brenda admitted that if it were up to her, they would have sex once every four weeks or so. She said, "I need time between sexual encounters to feel charged up again." To Brenda, this sexual downtime was not a problem. When Brenda and Bill made love, she thoroughly enjoyed it and had orgasms easily. She felt that Bill was a very good lover. Although Bill would have enjoyed more frequent sex, he was not particularly troubled by their lovemaking schedule.

If Wendy and Brenda had taken a standardized questionnaire assessing low sexual desire that asked about their ages, the number of years they

were married, health considerations, and the number of times they en-
gaged in sex each week, Wendy would have passed with flying colors.
Brenda, on the other hand, might have set the low-desire alarm ringing.
Yet, Wendy, not Brenda, was the one whose life had been affected nega-
tively by her level of desire. Although Brenda wasn't the world's most sex-
ual person, Bill wasn't either. That's why, despite the fact that Brenda and
Bill's sex life was less active than that of most other couples their age,
Brenda's sex drive was not a problem.

So, the first thing you should know about low sexual desire is that it really doesn't matter what your friends or neighbors are doing or what it
takes for other people to feel sexually satisfied. It's not about statistics. It's
about you and your spouse. If you think there's a problem, there's a problem. If your spouse is unhappy, there's a problem. Even if you're okay without sex, if your spouse is miserable and you want to stay married, you've
got a problem. You don't need to know much more than that. So throw
away your surveys. Stop looking for validation. Time to turn up the heat
in your relationship.

I assume that my telling you to become more proactive if *you're* unhappy makes perfect sense to you, but my second piece of advice—that
whether you're concerned about your low desire or not, you take your
spouse's feelings into account—may not be as easy to digest. After all, decisions about your own sexuality are so personal, they should be based
strictly on your own feelings and needs, right? It's your body. If you're not
in the mood, you're not in the mood. Is that how you have been thinking
about all of this? If so, fasten your seat belt because I'm going to whisk you
away from this kind of thinking as quickly as possible.

While it goes without saying that no one should engage in behavior,
sexual or otherwise, that is distasteful or demeaning, there are lots of really
good reasons you need to stretch yourself if you're the person with lower
desire. I'm going to tell you about those reasons. But before I do, I want to
reassure you that you aren't the only person who is going to have to
stretch; your spouse will too. There is no way your spouse will get through
this book without recognizing the role his or her actions might be playing in your sexual stalemate. I know that your marriage won't improve
unless your spouse changes too. However, for the moment, let's get back
to you.

THE SPOUSE WITH THE LOWER DESIRE SETS THE PACE

I'm focusing my efforts on you right now because it's been my observation that, just as in a classroom setting, the slowest child often determines the teacher's pace, in most relationships, the person with less interest in sex sets the rhythm and pace for the sexual relationship. You control when and how it happens (Schnarch, 1997). Of course, there are exceptions—the people who decide to "go along with the program" (an easier feat for women for obvious reasons) in order to avoid making waves. But generally, a steady diet of joyless, obligatory sex eventually results in marital disaster. And not much sex happens then.

If your marriage is like many others, your sexual relationship is probably shaped more by *your* level of desire and feelings about sex than by your spouse's. So in the end, although I will teach your spouse the things s/he needs to know about you, your feelings, and your sexuality, ultimately *you* have to be the one to take the primary responsibility for setting your sex drive on course. Your spouse can't force you to communicate more openly about your needs, go to a doctor, sex therapist, health club, try a new medication, or read a steamy romance novel. Only you are in charge of you. Even though your spouse has been trying to motivate you to change, at bottom, s/he knows if things are truly going to be different, it's ultimately in your hands. Your marriage depends on your taking this responsibility seriously.

So what am I saying here? Am I saying that you should have sex any time your spouse desires or that you should go through the motions just to keep peace? Hell, no! That's not what I'm saying at all. That sort of grin-and-bear-it sexual contact is meaningless, demeaning, and destructive. Healthy marriages depend on a loving sexual connection. Feelings of warmth, intimacy, closeness, and connectedness cannot grow in an environment that isn't rich with touch. If your lack of interest in being sexual with your spouse has prevented you from nurturing that part of your marriage, you need to do whatever it takes to fuel your desire so that you want and welcome sexuality into your marriage.

I'm also not talking about just having more sex. Although I feel pretty certain your spouse wouldn't complain if I told you to focus on making love more often, addressing the issues in your sex-starved marriage is more complex than that. Even if your spouse is complaining about infrequent sex, s/he is probably saying something much deeper: "You're not passionate." "You don't care about our relationship." "I'm not important to you." "I don't excite you." Agreeing to more frequent but no more genuine or enthusiastic a sexual connection will probably not quell these hurt feelings. You have to begin to think and feel differently about the role of sexuality in your life. If you want your marriage to improve and your sex drive to return in earnest, you are going to have to make a fundamental change in the way you approach your spouse, your marriage, and your sexuality. You are going to have to get inspired.

BUT I'M JUST NOT A SEXUAL PERSON

As you are reading this, are you saying to yourself, "I can't imagine what would pique my interest in sex. I'm just not a sexual person"? If so, it may be due to the fact that, without knowing it, you've been brainwashed by the conventional definition of sexual desire, which some experts now question. And if you have, you may not be as lukewarm to sex as you think.

Sexual desire is typically thought of as the first stage in a three-step process: desire, followed by arousal, and then orgasm. The thinking goes something like this. In the midst of your everyday activities, you have a sexual thought or fantasy prompted by a provocative photo, a sensual person, seductive words, an alluring scent, or just a random thought. You begin to feel turned on. This is considered sexual desire. Sexual desire then prompts you to initiate physical/sexual contact. You might become sexual with your spouse, or you might begin to masturbate.

As you continue to be stimulated physically, you start to feel aroused. If you're a woman, you notice a feeling of fullness in your pelvic area as your genitals become engorged with blood and your vagina begins lubricating. If you're a man, your penis becomes erect. As arousal increases, you reach orgasm—the rhythmic and pleasurable contractions that force blood to flow away from the pelvic area. Then gradually, your body returns to the nonaroused state.

So what's wrong with looking at the human sexual response cycle and in particular, desire, in this way? For one thing, this model assumes everyone experiences sexuality in a similar fashion—desire → arousal → orgasm → resolution—when, in fact, research suggests otherwise (Basson, 2001). Among other things, it appears that some people, particularly many women in long-term marriages, do not experience spontaneous or out-of-the-blue sexual thoughts or fantasies. However, when they decide to be receptive to their partners' advances or initiate sexual contact themselves, not to quell a sexual hunger but for other, equally valid reasons such as the desire for intimate connection, being touched in stimulating ways often leads to arousal. Arousal triggers a strong desire to continue being sexual. Hence, desire *follows* arousal.

Have you ever noticed that although you might not have been thinking sexual thoughts or feeling particularly sexy, if you push yourself to "get started" when your spouse approaches you, it feels good, and you find yourself getting into it? If so, this upside-down view of sexual desire can be incredibly liberating. It's not that you lack sexual desire, it's just that for you, desire doesn't happen until you've been physically aroused.

You need to stop thinking of yourself as someone who isn't sexual just because you don't daydream about sex or find yourself lusting after your partner while you're in the midst of reading your newspaper or working on the computer. It may just not be your style. If, however, when your spouse touches, kisses, and holds you, it feels good and increases your desire to continue connecting sexually, guess what? You're not desireless; you're filled with desire. Your body simply works differently. Stop comparing yourself to other people whose desire seems to just happen. You're different. Different isn't bad; it's just different.

I've often talked about this model of desire in workshops with couples and, inevitably someone, usually a man, raises his hand and comments, "I'm so glad you're saying this. My wife never seems to want sex. She's always too busy or preoccupied. But when I convince her to stop what she's doing, she always enjoys it. When we're done, I often joke with her and tell her to get out a magic marker and write on the back of her hand, 'I like sex,' so she doesn't forget it for the next time." The last time I shared this man's comment at another one of my workshops, another man said, "Forget the magic marker, I say, 'Get a tattoo.' " This desire follows arousal model fits for some men as well.

WHERE ARE THE FIREWORKS?

I have learned something else about people who tell themselves that they just aren't sexual people. Years ago, I attended a workshop on the topic of the desire gap in couples taught by my friend and colleague Dr. Pat Love. Among the many insightful and interesting nuggets I took away with me that day, one in particular stuck with me: that for some not-so-highly sexed people, although they do experience desire, it really isn't about fireworks, it's about flickering sparks. Instead of feeling dizzy with lust (as their partners might), some people simply have occasional sexual thoughts and feelings, so fleeting and subtle they often go unnoticed. Yet they're there.

I took this idea back with me to my office and from that day forward began to routinely ask self-avowed low-desire clients to pay more attention to their flickering sparks. As people became more aware of the subtle ways their minds and bodies signaled desire, their self-concept changed; they began to feel sexy again.

This sparks-versus-fireworks approach may be one that you will find useful. If you give yourself half a chance to discover the rumblings of sexual desire rather than wait for the big bang, you may surprise yourself. You might discover that when you listen harder to your mind and body, the signals have been there all along. The reception just hasn't been very good up until now, but you can fix that.

BUT WHAT IF I'M STILL NOT IN THE MOOD?
THEN WHAT?

The next two chapters will help you get a better handle on the various paths you can take to boost your desire. But before we go there, I want you to think about something. Desiring your spouse sexually isn't always about sexual gratification. But why in the world would a person choose to be sexual if sexual gratification isn't the driving force? This is a very important question that truly challenges many of the basic notions on which conventional thinking about sexuality are based. Let me backtrack for a moment.

It is often assumed that love is at the core of people's decisions to get and stay married. How incredibly shortsighted and naive! People decide to get married and remain committed to their partners for many, many reasons, not just love alone. (In fact, most people in long-term marriages have those days when they even wonder, "What's love got to do with it?") Some of these reasons, though less romantic and considerably more pragmatic—to bear and raise children, pool financial resources, have a sexual partner, companion, and someone to grow old with, combat loneliness and fear of the unknown, and so on—are nonetheless less equally valid and important.

Similarly, it is absurd to assume that the only reason people desire sex is to satisfy a biological urge. Human beings are incredibly complex. Although biology undoubtedly influences our sexuality, it is but one among many other factors. When people decide to become sexual, they do so for a variety of reasons besides seeking sexual gratification. They become sexual to feel close emotionally during and/or after sex, to enhance intimacy in general, to please one's partner, to relax, to feel "sexual" or attractive, to express attraction, to reconcile, to procreate, and so on.

If you've been thinking that the only good reason to make love or be physical with your spouse is if you feel turned on sexually, think again. Look at your sexual relationship from a broader perspective. If, for example, you value how being sexually in sync brings you closer to your spouse, or how pleasing your spouse gives you pleasure, or how your tender touches when you're making love can so aptly say, "I'm sorry," or "I want you," then you'll have lots of reasons to "just say yes."

SEX AND TOUCHING OFTEN GO HAND IN HAND

When couples are feeling good about each other and their sexual relationship, they are often physically affectionate as well. And they're fortunate!

There is little that is more soothing or reassuring than a gentle caress. Touch does what words cannot. We've learned from animal studies and from babies who are raised in touch-deprived environments that the young of many species fail to thrive and even die without the comfort of touch.

> Touching is a basic animal instinct. Nature seems to have designed it that way. We crave the emotional nutrition that comes from touch, just like an essential vitamin. . . . The truth is, we can't live without it. We develop a form of emotional scurvy, although we call it by different terms: depression, stress, anxiety, aggression, and midlife crisis . . . and treat it with drugs that don't work. Lack of touch is just as detrimental to our health as a lack of vitamin C and just as easy to remedy. (Gochros, 1980)

Unfortunately, when sex becomes a problem in relationships, many couples tell me that they stop touching each other altogether. They don't hold hands, snuggle on the couch, rub each other's backs or feet, or even hug when they part. This is an enormous price to pay.

A GOOD SEXUAL RELATIONSHIP MAKES YOU FEEL CLOSE EMOTIONALLY

Show me a couple who has a mutually satisfying sexual relationship, and I'll show you a couple I can pick out of a crowd. There's an almost visible bond between them—the gentle touches, knowing glances, laughter, and warmth when their eyes meet. You can feel the connection between them.

Sex creates an incredibly powerful bond on many different levels. Not every sexual encounter leads to earth-shattering orgasms, or even consistent orgasms, for that matter. Nor will each and every sexual experience make you feel like soulmates. But the best way to ensure a strong emotional and spiritual bond with your spouse is to do the one thing that defines your relationship as different from all others: stay sexually connected.

SEX PRODUCES "FEEL GOOD" CHEMICALS

When you're in the throes of passion, your body releases chemicals that make you feel good, such as endorphins and oxytocin. Endorphins are nature's opiates; they protect you from pain and give you a sense of well-being. Runners often refer to "the runner's high"—an endorphin-induced euphoric feeling they have after running for a period of time. If you're a woman who has breast-fed her children, perhaps you're familiar with oxytocin—the hormone that allows you to relax so that your milk flows. But it has another function: it increases sensitivity to touch and is sometimes referred to as the bonding hormone. It creates a feeling of connectedness between a mother and her baby. In marriage, in addition to creating a feeling of calmness and connectedness between you and your spouse, oxytocin also triggers orgasm. "Feel good" chemicals are at work when we make love.

MARRIAGE IS A TWO-WAY STREET

I've saved the best and most important reason to improve your sexual relationship for last: marriage is a two-way street. People who truly understand this principle take it to heart and practice it, and grow old together. They cherish each other. They become soulmates. People who don't become bitter, cynical, selfish, and lonely. See for yourself.

The following is a conversation between two real people:

JENNIFER: Are you willing to go with me to counseling to try to resolve these issues?

RICK: If that's what it takes for you to be told that you are being unreasonable, then, yes, I'll go.

JENNIFER: Please tell me what you think I want that is unreasonable.

RICK: All this talk about sex and affection is ridiculous. I work hard all day, and I shouldn't then have to fight you off. After twenty-four years, you should just know I love you. I shouldn't have to go through a bunch of BS to pacify you.

JENNIFER: So you think it's unreasonable for me to expect affection, hugs, and passionate kisses once in a while?

RICK: After twenty-four years, yes.

JENNIFER: I'm afraid that counseling wouldn't do us any good if you are going with such a closed mind, but let me ask you this. If our therapist suggested that we see a sex therapist, what would you say?

RICK: Hell, no!! I'm not paying someone $150 to tell me that I need to set aside special time for us. I'm not interested in sex anymore, not with you or any other woman. It's over. I don't want or need it, and if you can't accept that, then you need to leave.

JENNIFER: Would you at least be willing to listen to what a professional has to say?

RICK: *No!* I will go to a regular counselor and let them tell *you* that you are wrong, but I won't discuss sex. Period.

JENNIFER: What if I said right now that I can't live like this anymore; I need more from you. I love you, and you are the man I want to be intimate with, to share quiet, cozy moments with, to connect to, but if you won't meet me halfway then I am leaving.

RICK: Leave.

This dialogue takes my breath away. I feel incredibly sad when I read it. I can't imagine what it would be like to be in Jennifer's shoes. It must feel like a stabbing pain in her heart. Rick has complete disregard for what's important to Jennifer. They're about to become another divorce statistic.

I've heard some version of this interaction many times over the years. It's truly unfortunate. You can't make a marriage work if all you care about is what makes *you* happy. Good marriages are about both spouses being happy, and this involves compromise. Although most people acknowledge the importance of compromising about childrearing decisions, restaurant choices, where to spend the holidays, who's going to take out the garbage, or whose responsibility it is to empty the litter box, sex usually isn't thought of in this way. Since sex is such a personal issue, we generally assume that the decision to have it or decline should be strictly a personal one. But the truth is, there isn't any aspect of your life together that is exempt from this very basic relationship rule: the key to loving marriages is real giving.

REAL GIVING

In most relationships, people have a mistaken notion about giving. We tend to give to others in the way we ourselves like to receive. If we like our spouses to give us space and privacy when we're down and out, we tend to treat our spouses similarly when they're down in the dumps. If we are extremely sentimental and romantic about holidays and birthdays, we tend to be extravagant gift givers on special days.

But what if our spouses prefer sharing feelings rather than be given space when they're upset? Is it really a gift to back off and let them sulk alone? And what if our spouses are less romantic and really prefer that no fuss be made over their birthdays and holidays? Is it really a gift to give flashy presents and sappy Hallmark™ cards? I think not. Let me take this a step further.

When it comes to feeling loved in a marriage, everybody has different requirements. Some people feel loved when their spouses spend time with them. Others feel loved when they have had good talks. A spouse's kind deeds—pouring a cup of coffee, making a favorite meal, warming up a cold car in advance—can, for some, prompt feelings of love and connection. For many, touch says love like no other. Making love *is* love. You may be married to one of those people. And if so, try as you may to express love your way—by doing kind things, fixing the vacuum cleaner, handling the lion's share of the child care, paying the bills, being available for heart-to-heart talks, earning lots of money, becoming a gourmet cook, and so on—your words and actions will fall on deaf ears and deaf hearts. If you're married to someone who feels your love through touch and, in particular, your sexual relationship, unless you love him or her in this way, you aren't really loving. You aren't doing real giving.

Real giving is when you give to your spouse not what *you* want or need but that which *your spouse* wants and needs. Plus—and this part is really important—you don't really have to fully understand why your spouse feels the way s/he does. You don't have to agree with it. You just have to do it. That's what real giving is all about.

People in long-term loving marriages do real giving all the time. They're wise enough to realize the benefits of it. Giving, especially if they have to stretch themselves to do it, makes them feel good about themselves. They get pleasure in giving pleasure. The other reason is that they get a whole lot back in return. Love is contagious. When you give genuinely and consistently, your spouse will reciprocate. S/he will want to make you happy, to please you. That's the way it works the vast majority of the time.

So whether you're doing it for you, your spouse, your marriage, or all of the above, when you begin to reap the benefits of bringing back the passion in your marriage, it will leave you wondering, "Why did I wait so long?"

CHAPTER THREE

What's Causing My Desire Doldrums?

Now that you have a better understanding about what low desire really is, I want you to know a little more about its many causes. Although in this chapter, as in the previous one, I will be talking to the spouse with lower desire, if you're the more highly sexed spouse, don't disappear. You need to read this chapter as well because it will help you understand the reasons your spouse is feeling as s/he does.

There is a great deal of information in this chapter. However, when it comes to understanding the full range of reasons people lose interest in sex, I have only scratched the surface. I make no bones about it; it is not my intent to offer you *The Complete Encyclopedia of the Causes of Low Sexual Desire.* Instead, I want to give you enough information about potential causes for the drop in your libido so that you can begin to see that there are many potential solutions.

And speaking of solutions, although it might be tempting to skip this chapter entirely and go directly to Chapter 4 on solutions, don't do it. Once you become clearer about why you're feeling what you're feeling, you will be in a better position to decide what to do next. Start here.

Dear Michele,

Lately, I have absolutely no desire for sex. I have no idea why this is happening to me. I love my wife, and we get along just fine. I remember the good old days when I used to think, "I just can't wait to get into bed with her," but I haven't felt that for a long, long time. I can hardly even remember what that felt like. If it were left up to me, I'm not sure we'd ever have sex again. I'm too uncomfortable to talk to anyone about this, so please help explain what's going on here.

George

Sex is everywhere. It's on so-called family-oriented sit-coms, it's on drivetime radio, it's on the cover of *Sports Illustrated,* it sells newspapers; it's everywhere you look. In a culture where you can't escape sex even if you want to, feeling lustless is bound to evoke a variety of unsettling feelings. This is especially true if you can recall times in your life when you felt sexier and more passionate. Most people can. If this is true for you, perhaps you're asking yourself, "Why am I feeling this way?" There are lots of different reasons you might have lost your desire or feel sexually unresponsive. Sexual desire is fueled by a complex mix of biological, psychological, cultural, and relationship issues.

THE BIOLOGY OF DESIRE

A great deal has been learned about the role that a host of biological factors play—hormones, medications, and illnesses, for example—in a person's desire for sex. We also are learning an enormous amount about the way people's bodies function during sex. This information has given researchers a better handle on the mechanics of healthy sexual responses. Researchers are now better able to identify whether the "sexual machinery" is in working order and if not, why not. Why is this important?

When your body isn't functioning properly and sex isn't an enjoyable experience, it's easy to see why you would eventually stop desiring it. And apparently, there is no shortage of people experiencing sexual problems. According to a large study published in the *Journal of the American Medical Association,* slightly less than a third of women said they regularly didn't have orgasms and 23 percent said sex wasn't pleasurable. About a third of men said they had persistent problems with climaxing too early. Overall, 43 percent of women and 31 percent of men said they had one or more persistent problems with sex (Laumann, Paik, and Rosen, 1999).

Women's sexual problems tend to decrease with age (with the exception of problems with lubrication), whereas the opposite is true for men. Older men, fifty to fifty-nine years old, are three times more likely to experience erection problems than younger men. Following are some of the major sexual problems that can affect sexual desire.

Sexual Problems in Women

PROBLEMS WITH AROUSAL

Women experiencing sexual arousal disorders do not feel excitement or pleasure when sexually stimulated. This may be due to inadequate stimulation—her partner's not knowing how to touch her so that she feels aroused or her not knowing her own body well enough in order to instruct him—or physiological factors such as a lack of adequate blood flow to the genital area or an inability to lubricate sufficiently.

Although a lack of adequate blood flow can occur for various reasons, some women who have had hysterectomies experience this problem due to injury to nerves and blood vessels. It's also important for you to know that increased stimulation may be required to achieve arousal as people age. Sexual arousal problems can also be due to emotional or psychological factors such as depression or pent-up resentment. It's hard to relax and enjoy yourself when you're feeling blue or seeing red.

Sally, a fifty-four-year-old woman, was very concerned about her sex drive. Until recently, she and her husband had always had a very satisfying sexual relationship. They had made love two or three times a week for most of their twenty-nine-year marriage. However, in the last four months prior to my meeting her, orgasms were few and far between, and she found herself wanting sex less and less. Although she still enjoyed the physical contact with her husband when they made love, having never had problems achieving orgasms before, she felt confused and worried. "Michele," she said, "I've been wondering whether there's something wrong with me or my marriage."

I asked Sally about many different aspects of their lovemaking, health issues, her lifestyle, and their relationship, but when I asked, "In the last four months, when you have had orgasms, what was different about those times?" we discovered something that proved interesting. After some thought, Sally said, "I recall two times in particular. The first orgasm occurred after my husband and I had made love for a much longer time than we usually do. I was determined not to give up, and he seemed okay with that. My orgasm was great, just like in the good old days."

I asked Sally about the second experience. She told me, "Every once in a while, my husband and I like to use a vibrator. After weeks of not having an orgasm, I decided to try something new, so I used my vibrator. I had an orgasm pretty quickly after that."

First, I talked to Sally about the importance of not always being so goal oriented in her lovemaking. We talked about ways she could focus on the pleasurable aspects of their connecting physically without her feeling the need to have an orgasm each and every time they made love. Then we did a little detective work and talked about the similarity in the two times she was able to have an orgasm: she received more stimulation. I reassured Sally that this is a common need for many people as they age.

Sally was relieved on several counts. Our discussion made her realize that although her orgasms weren't as frequent as before, she was still able to experience them. Plus, she now knew what she could do to increase the frequency of her orgasms even more if she so desired. She also realized that her lack of regular orgasms was not a sign that something was wrong with her marriage. She later told me that feeling reassured about her marriage enabled her to relax, which seemed to improve things even more.

PROBLEMS WITH ORGASMS

When women have orgasmic disorders, they are unable to achieve orgasm after sufficient sexual stimulation and excitement. Included in this category are women who have never experienced orgasm, as well as those who have recurrent and persistent difficulties in doing so. *Orgasmic disorder* also refers to women who become distressed due to *any* difficulty in achieving orgasm. For example, some women who in the past experienced relatively strong orgasms but currently experience only mild ones fit this description.

SEXUAL PAIN DISORDERS

Sexual pain disorders include dyspareunia (recurrent or persistent genital pain that accompanies sexual intercourse) and vaginismus (a recurrent or persistent involuntary spasm of the vagina wall that interferes with penetration or intercourse).

Male Sexual Problems

EJACULATION DISORDERS

The simplest way to think about ejaculation disorders is that ejaculations can happen "before you want them, when you want them, not as soon as you want them, or not at all" (Gochros and Fischer, 1980). The number one male sexual complaint is premature ejaculation (PE)—when ejaculation occurs before or soon after penetration. Men experiencing PE feel as if they have little or no control over the timing of their ejaculations. Since sexual performance during intercourse is often the yardstick by which men measure their sexual prowess, ejaculating earlier than desired often leads to shame, frustration, and sometimes avoidance of sexual encounters.

ERECTILE DYSFUNCTION

Erectile dysfunction (ED) is the inability to achieve or maintain an erection long enough to have mutually satisfying intercourse. ED is quite common; most men experience it at some point in their lives. Unless it is chronic or recurrent, it is usually not problematic. Although aging makes erectile dysfunction more likely—52 percent of men aged forty to seventy and even higher percentages in older men—it is by no means an inevitability, even in seventy- and eighty-year-old men.

ED can be primary—a man has never been able to get or maintain an erection—or, more likely, secondary—a man could previously function satisfactorily but no longer can. Secondary ED often has underlying biological causes, such as vascular problems, hormonal disorders, drug use, or neurologic disorders.

But regardless of what causes ED initially, when a man feels distressed by his inability to satisfy himself or his partner, secondary problems of a psychological nature often develop. Anxiety, depression, and, ultimately, sexual avoidance are frequently the result.

Physiological Causes of Low Desire

If frustrating sexual problems are causing you to be less interested in your sexual relationship with your spouse, Chapter 4 will help you decide on the steps that you should take. And now to the physiological causes of low desire.

Although it's important to identify any biological or physiological factors influencing your low libido, keep in mind that a drop in sexual desire is rarely caused by physiological factors alone. There is almost always an emotional overlay when it comes to problems with sexual desire. Therefore, even if physiological factors are a main contributing factor to your low sexual desire, unless you also address the other complex personal and relationship issues that might be affecting you (even if these issues arose because of chronic physiological problems), these concerns will remain unresolved and dampen chances for any real improvement in your sexual relationship. If, after reading the information about biological factors, you want to learn more, I will refer you to other, more in-depth information on this subject.

HORMONES RUNNING AMOK

If you're a woman or you're married to one, I'm certain that you don't need anyone to tell you that hormones affect how people think, feel, and behave. If nothing else, you know that there must be some good explanation for the moodiness and tender breasts that occur around "that time of month." A woman in my practice recently told me, "When I get PMS, I see my life through negative lenses: my husband is rotten, the kids are unappreciative, my job stinks, and my friends always disappoint me. After my period, everything is just fine."

But what you might not know is that fluctuating hormones may be one of the reasons you aren't sexually inclined. For example, some people have below-normal levels of testosterone, one of the primary hormones regulating sex drive *in both men and women*. When you have sufficient testosterone in your bloodstream to do the work it's supposed to do, most people feel vibrant, sexy, have sexual thoughts throughout the day, and find themselves fantasizing from time to time. Without sufficient amounts of this hormone, your sexual desire can fade or become nonexistent.

When testosterone levels are abnormally low and people's sex drives plummet, sometimes they incorrectly assume something is flawed about their marriages or their lives. This is extremely unfortunate. A person with a testosterone deficiency might lose desire for sex even if s/he were married to the perfect person oozing with sex appeal.

Probably one of the most common and troublesome examples of this is what happens in the early years of a relationship when infatuation is the rule:

> Let's say that a high-T and a low-T person (someone with either high or low levels of testosterone) become attracted to one another (highly likely since opposites attract). During infatuation, with the help of PEA [phenethylamine], dopamine, and norepinephrine, the person with the low sex drive (the low-T person) experiences a surge in sexual desire. While under the influence of the love cocktail, the low-T person thinks, feels, and acts like a high-T person. This individual who ordinarily has little interest in sex, who is not easily aroused and doesn't think about sex, experiences just the opposite. On any given day, sexual fantasies, love play, and sexual initiation all become part of the infatuated behavior of the low-T lover, who is now believing "I have finally found someone who turns me on." Meanwhile, the high-T person is thinking, "I have died and gone to heaven. I have finally found someone who enjoys sex as much as I do." (Love, 2001, pp. 45–46)

Over time, the impact of these hormones fades, and both spouses return to their normal levels of sexual interest, leaving the high-T person feeling duped and deceived, the low-T person questioning himself or herself or, more commonly, the relationship.

Fluctuating levels of testosterone aren't the only reason people lose desire. A delicate balance of other equally important hormones must be maintained in order for your sex drive to thrive. Although hormone imbalances can happen at any time in life, here are some common triggering events:

Childbirth: It is completely normal for women to experience a drop in desire following the birth of a baby. The fatigue and physical discomfort following delivery often make sex less appealing. Additionally, prolactin, the hormone that stimulates milk production in nursing women, is known to suppress estrogen and testosterone. A drop in estrogen can cause vaginal dryness, making intercourse uncomfortable. Countless women complain of having low sexual desire, not just immediately following the birth of their children but for years after as well.

Menopause: Menopause marks a significant transition in a woman's life. Research suggests that approximately 40 percent of women lose desire during this time in their lives (Reichman, 1998, p. 31). During menopause, women experience a significant drop in estrogen, which often creates a thinning of the vaginal walls and difficulties with lubrication, again making intercourse uncomfortable. There is also reduced blood flow to the genitals, which can result in arousal difficulties. Some women begin to have more difficulty achieving orgasm, and when they do, they find their orgasms aren't quite as strong as before. Testosterone production slows, and that decreases desire and sexual fantasies. Other testosterone deficiency symptoms are depression, headaches, and a loss of general sense of well-being, all of which go a long way to decreasing sexual desire. If you're a woman who is not quite of menopausal age, the drop in your desire may still be hormonally related. Menopause doesn't happen all of a sudden; it occurs gradually. The period preceding menopause is called *perimenopause.* Research indicates that 30 percent of women feel less sexually inclined during perimenopause.

Male menopause: Although everyone knows about menopause in women, many experts believe that men go through a comparable transition as they age; it's referred to as "male menopause" or "andropause." Andropause involves hormonal and physiological changes in men ages forty to fifty-five, though many say that it can occur as early as thirty-five or as late as sixty-five. This stage is often characterized by a drop in testosterone and other hormones such as dopamine, oxytocin, vasopressin, melatonin, DHEA, and pregnenolone. These hormonal changes often lead to depression, weight gain, and a decreased sex drive—the most common symptom. And believe it or not, many "menopausal" men experience hot flashes, sweats, depression, nervousness, and fatigue just as women do.

Medications, Illnesses, and Unhealthy Substances

In addition to hormone fluctuations, there are other physiological causes of low sexual desire such as:

- Side effects from commonly prescribed medications such as antidepressants, antihypertensives, antihistamines, tranquilizers, and birth control pills
- Side effects of chemotherapy
- The impact of chronic diseases or other underlying medical conditions, such as liver, kidney, or pituitary disease, diabetes, hypothyroidism, cardiovascular disease, Parkinson's disease, endocrine and neurological disorders, anemia, and arthritis
- Alcohol, tobacco, or illegal substances such as heroin, cocaine, and marijuana
- Physical disability or chronic pain

*　　*　　*

As you read through some of the biological causes for low sexual desire, perhaps you were thinking, "Hm, this could be easy. Maybe it's just a matter of balancing my hormones or getting a prescription of Viagra." And maybe you're right. But before you convince yourself that you are testosterone deprived or that some other biological problem is the only cause of the dip in your desire, keep reading, because the plot thickens.

PSYCHOLOGICAL FACTORS AND DESIRE

People with low desire often say that the sky could be falling, but it doesn't stop their spouses from wanting sex. But not so with you. You've got to be in a positive frame of mind to get your juices flowing. And a myriad of psychological issues can leave you otherwise preoccupied or disengaged.

Depression

Everyone gets blue once in a while; that's to be expected. However, if you've been feeling down for several weeks or longer, you might be clinically depressed, and if so, your sexual appetite is often the first thing to go. Depression affects approximately 20 to 30 million Americans, making it the most common psychological problem in America.

Feeling depressed often interrupts your sleep, makes you feel listless and unmotivated, leaves you feeling weepy or numb, and takes away your appetite or prompts you to overindulge, eating everything in sight. Depressed people usually don't enjoy or seek out the company of others. Seventy-five percent of people who are depressed report a loss of sex drive. And oddly enough, people who are depressed are sometimes the last ones to recognize it. They often become defensive when loved ones express concern.

To make matters worse, if you do decide to get help in the form of antidepressants, many of them such as Prozac or Paxil, can themselves cause sexual dysfunctions, such as problems with arousal, orgasm, or ejaculation or erectile difficulties. You need to choose your treatment options carefully.

If you haven't been feeling yourself, you need to do something about it. If your spouse or other loved ones have told you that you seem depressed, trust them. They may be right. Get some help. Your marriage depends on it.

Sexual, Physical, or Emotional Abuse as a Child

The incidence of people who were molested or sexually abused as children is quite high. People who have had traumatic experiences as children sometimes carry unresolved feelings about these experiences into their relationships with their spouses. They have a hard time leaving the past in the past. Intimacy feels threatening and unappealing. Some people even have flashbacks during sexual encounters. For many, sex feels like something to avoid rather than pursue.

Poor Self-Esteem

Bette Midler once said, "I dislike myself so much, if I could break the date with myself, I would." Many people are their own worst critics. They demand perfection and get down on themselves when they come up short. If you compare yourself to others and feel that you're always the runner-up, if you're unhappy with your lot in life or your accomplishments, if you're in a rut and find yourself ruminating about your failures, you're probably not going to too much energy or desire for sex. When you're feeling crappy about you, it puts a damper on your outlook on everything, including being sexual.

Body Image

Do you know anyone who can honestly say that s/he is happy with his or her body? I don't. Most people are experts on their obvious and not-so-obvious body flaws. They feel shame and disgust. They avoid being naked. Sexual experiences are filled with anxiety and embarrassment. And who wants to do *that* on a regular basis?

Are you unhappy with your body? Do you think your breasts and other body parts are too little or too big? Do you think your penis or your biceps should be bigger and your stomach flatter? Do you have a hard time relaxing when you're naked because you're so self-conscious about the fact that you've gained weight? If the answer to these questions is yes, then you need to know that poor body image is a definite desire squelcher, and you need to take a crash course in self-acceptance or do something to change things.

Grief over a Loss

If you've experienced a death of a loved one—a relative, a friend, or even a pet—the grief that often follows can be all-consuming and even incapacitating. This is true of other losses as well, such as the loss of a job or the breakup of an important relationship.

In the early stages of grief, it is hard to think about anything other than your loss. Your intense sorrow and anger can have a numbing effect. You begin to wonder whether you'll ever snap out of it. Sadness and grief after a loss are to be expected, but sometimes grief can keep an incapacitating grip for far too long. When this happens, it interferes with normal functioning and joy in life.

If you have lost a loved one or experienced a major disappointment and you find yourself thinking about this person or situation much of the time, it may definitely be zapping your interest in sex.

Motherhood

Beyond the hormonal changes that occur when women give birth, there are often psychological changes that lower a woman's desire for sex. Many women say that once they have children, they feel changed. They feel like moms, not sexual beings. Unless a woman understands the importance of adapting to her changing role as both mother and wife, she may start focusing all of her attention on her children and neglect all aspects of her marital relationship.

Midlife Crisis

Although people usually think that a midlife crisis is a "man's thing," I meet many women who could give any man going through this stage a run for his money. So whether you're male or female, the following description might apply.

Many people wake up one morning and realize for the first time that they aren't going to live forever. They notice their bodies aging. They have wrinkles in new places. Their wrinkles have wrinkles. Their waists are growing. Their hair is graying, thinning, or altogether gone. Reading glasses have become an annoying necessity. The little aches and pains in their joints and other body parts are the main topic of conversation with friends. It all adds up to a very depressing epiphany: "I'm middle-aged."

Suddenly, there's this scary awareness: "Life is passing me by." It is then that many people begin to soul-search or take inventory of their lives. Am I happy? Have I accomplished everything I hoped to accomplish in my life? What would bring me more joy? Is my marriage helping or hindering my personal growth and satisfaction? And although you know the old cliché—the red convertible, ferocious workouts at the gym, a brand-new, seductive wardrobe, plastic surgery, and the dawning of a passion for music revered by people half your age—what you might not know is that many people in the midst of this personal introspection start questioning their marriage. They wonder if their spouses are at the root of their existential angst. And while they wonder, sex with one's spouse often goes right out the window.

Fatigue

There's no question about it. Our lives are hectic. We take care of kids. We work overtime. We clean, cook, coach soccer practice, and sing in the choir. We volunteer and have holidays at our house. We pay bills and make sure we have time to call our aging relatives. Our lives are so busy that we can hardly breathe. And then we wonder why we're just plain pooped. We've got nothing left to give. Just the thought of becoming sexual feels like a chore.

Stress

Whether you're stressed about work, your family, or other aspects of your life, you should know that stress isn't just in your head. Stress takes its toll on your body. It makes sleep hard to come by. Your energy level takes a dip. It weakens your immune system, and you often become ill. Your body often starts hurting as if to say, "Help, slow down!" You are on overload. You feel frazzled and tense much of the time. Nothing seems like fun anymore, not even sex. When sex starts feeling like a chore, it often gets moved to the last chore on your to-do list.

CULTURAL EXPECTATIONS

There are cultural reasons you might not yearn for or enjoy sex. When you were growing up, you might have learned certain ideas from your parents, religious training, or society in general that have made enjoyable sex more of a challenge.

Children are like sponges, absorbing and believing much of what adults tell them about the world. If you were taught that sex is bad or dirty or that you're a bad person for thinking about sex, chances are that these ideas have become a part of you. Many adults have to unlearn their childhood lessons in order to relax and truly enjoy themselves. Here are some of the most common sexual myths that pass down through our culture, generation from generation:

> Good girls don't have sex.
> Guys who desire sex are macho, but girls who want sex are nymphos, easy, or sluts.
> Sex is for procreation, not enjoyment.
> Women should never appear too interested.
> When women say no, they really mean yes.
> The bigger a man's penis, the better a sexual partner.
> Intercourse is what sex is really about.
> Masturbation is bad.

Sex is a natural, wonderful, and pleasurable experience. It should feel relaxing and enjoyable. If, during your intimate moments with your spouse, you feel bad about yourself or shamed about your actions, it's possible that you are still under the influence of powerful lessons of the past. You can learn how to shake free from these scripts so that you can reclaim your sexuality and discover sexual fulfillment.

*   *   *

Do any of these psychological issues ring true for you? Did you see yourself in any of the descriptions? If so, pay particular attention to the solutions devoted to resolving personal issues in the next chapter. If not, relationship issues may be more of what is driving your problems with low desire. But before we begin examining your marriage, consider the following.

I have worked with many people who experience the enervating emotions I just described but are so busy doing what's required of them and going through the motions that they aren't really tuned into their inner feelings. They don't realize they're clinically depressed. They don't know that their stress levels are off the charts. They ignore the fact that a loved one's death has had a much greater impact on them than they ever suspected. They assume their self-hate about their imperfect bodies is something they just have to live with.

And, if your spouse has been playing amateur psychologist and telling you that s/he knows (better than you) the reason your desire has evaporated—"You're not into sex because _____ [you're depressed, you don't like your body]," I can see why you might have become defensive. But as I told you before, I am going to get your spouse to back off and give you space to think this through with an open heart. The truth is, if you've been down, stressed out, tired, plagued by unpleasant thoughts about the past, or having a "bad body day," you will need to face it and confront it head-on if you're hoping to rouse your feelings of sexuality once again.

If you really don't believe that personal issues are getting in the way of more enjoyable sex, then perhaps there's a different reason you're feeling what you're feeling: your marriage is a trouble spot.

RELATIONSHIP ISSUES

Although relationship issues are last on this list, I can tell you with confidence that last is definitely not least in terms of importance. In order to feel turned on, most people need to feel good about their marriage. If you're upset with your spouse for any number of reasons, your desire will probably wane. Anger, resentment, disappointment, hurt, or betrayal dampen most people's desire. Here are some questions to ask yourself about your marriage.

Do you find yourself frequently rehashing (in your own mind or out loud) your spouse's past hurtful action?

Do you try to address troublesome issues but feel that your spouse shuts you out?

Do you often feel your spouse is very unsupportive of you and your feelings?

Do you see your spouse as controlling or critical much of the time, and does this anger you?

Do your spouse's actions frequently disappoint you, but you keep your
feelings to yourself?

If you answer yes to any of these questions, negative feelings are probably holding you back from wanting to be closer to your spouse. You will
need to address the issues bothering you. Although the next chapter will
offer you some tools on tackling these issues in constructive ways, let's
take a closer look at some of the most common passion busters right now.

Going Along with the Program

When two people live under the same roof, it's inevitable that there will be
disagreement and conflict. It's the nature of all relationships. The people
we marry aren't our clones, and we will not see eye-to-eye all the time.
And thank God for that. It would be incredibly boring if we did! However,
conflict is tricky business. People who learn how to manage it have loving,
caring, and intimate relationships. People who don't, don't. They either
fight constantly (and I'll tell you more about these people next), or they
avoid conflict at any cost.

Some people are so determined to ward off conflict that no matter how
much they disagree with their spouses or are unhappy with their marriages, they keep things inside. They swallow bad feelings. They're determined to avoid getting their spouses angry and having to endure their
wrath.

Compulsive conflict avoiders usually think they're helping matters by
keeping their feelings inside. But the truth is, they're destroying themselves and they're taking their marriages down with them. It's impossible
to regularly stuff negative feelings about your spouse and his or her actions
without killing any desire for connection, both emotional and physical. It
just can't be done. Resentment and anger lie just below the surface every
waking minute of every day. Good times are viewed as being in denial.

The Assertiveness Trap

Now that I've told you how keeping unhappy feelings inside can ruin your
desire to be close to your spouse, I also need to caution you about the as-

sertiveness trap. I've seen countless people who, when they finally wake up to the fact that they've been spineless marshmallow spouses, swing the pendulum with all their might and take a stand on *everything*. A wet towel on the floor or a ten-minute late arrival for dinner spurs anger equal in magnitude to inappropriate flirting at a party with a neighbor. Your entire marriage is placed under a microscope, and any infraction, mild or otherwise, prompts an immediate "I'm angry and I'm not going to take it anymore" reaction.

Here's something you ought to know: when it comes to marriage, this sort of tell-it-like-it-is modus operandi is a formula for disaster. It's unfair and unrealistic, and will leave you (not to mention your spouse) feeling angry most of the time—not exactly an aphrodisiac.

Lack of Forgiveness

If conflict is inevitable in every marriage, then one of the primary skills every married person requires is the ability to make up and forgive. Everybody fights, but not everybody knows how to let go of the bad feelings that usually accompany arguments. Some people hang on to feelings of hurt and anger forever. They keep score. The smallest unkind or thoughtless deed prompts a regurgitating of a laundry list a mile long of past failings. In my years as a marriage therapist, I can tell you with confidence that holding grudges is one of the most effective methods for killing desire that I've ever seen.

Sometimes letting go of the past feels like an impossible feat, especially when the hurt is enormous. Betrayal such as infidelity can threaten the very foundation on which marriages are based. Letting go, moving on, and being intimate again are incredibly challenging tasks.

If your sexual desire has plummeted because of a major betrayal, if you haven't been able to resolve important issues with your spouse so that you can get back to loving each other again, you need to get some help.

Low Sexual IQ

To desire something, it must be enjoyable. If sex isn't pleasurable or if it's downright boring, you will stop wanting it. Sometimes sex isn't pleasurable because one or both spouses don't know how to turn their partners on. They don't have adequate sexual skills, and they're lacking solid, useful information about how their bodies work.

Part of the problem is that, contrary to what people believe, good sex doesn't just happen. You may be biologically programmed to have sex, but you're not biologically programmed to have a *satisfying* sex life. You've got to learn along the way. But because people often assume they should know everything there is to know about sex, when sexual problems occur, they think the problems are the result of bad relationships or health problems as opposed to a simple lack of skills. If your sexual relationship isn't satisfying, before you read too much into it, start reading some of the books in my bibliography at the end of the book. You'll be better off.

Sex-Talk Phobia

I know I should be used to it by now, but I'm not. I can't get over how many couples, despite decades of marriage, having raised children together, smelled each other's breath in the morning, seen one another in their most unbecoming lights, yet feel mortified, even petrified, by the idea of talking about sex! It's amazing! When I ask these couples about their touching, kissing, or lovemaking, embarrassment and fear are written all over their faces.

It would be easy to assume, as I did initially, that their apprehension was due to the fact that I, a perfect stranger, was asking them to divulge incredibly personal information. Sometimes this was so. However, many of these couples confessed that they never talked to each other in the privacy of their bedrooms! After years of marriage, they were too embarrassed. Yikes! How can you be intimate with someone and not talk about your intimate acts?

I have seen great things happen in marriages when people finally start talking. Misunderstandings clear. Goodwill returns. And when you pair a willingness to talk more openly about sex with an interest in boosting your sexual IQ, problems with sexual desire often become a thing of the past.

The Intimacy Dilemma

Beyond the sticky relationship issues, there is a more pervasive reason millions of people lose desire. It has to do with differences in the way many men and women think about and achieve intimacy. If there were ever a gender gap, this is it. As you read about this phenomenon, keep in mind that it is a generalization, and as with most other generalizations and stereotypes, it may be different in your marriage. If so, just substitute the words, *man* for *woman,* or *his* for *her* and vice versa. Don't get hung up on the fact that I'm generalizing. Take what applies to you and leave the rest.

THE CATCH-22

If you're a woman, and you're like many other women, you need to feel close to your husband emotionally in order to desire him physically. And for you, being close entails spending time together and engaging in meaningful conversation. It means feeling more important than his work, sports, buddies, and computer time. It requires discussions that delve much deeper than the pragmatic, "Who's-going-to-drive-the-kids-to-ballet-lesson-today?" or "What's-for-dinner?" For you, intimate conversations are like foreplay. A woman's libido can often be measured by her husband's willingness to get close "woman style." It's a rather simple formula that not enough highly sexed men know.

But there's a flip side to this formula. Many men don't seem to get the same charge out of talking that women do. It's not that men don't have a need to be close to other people. They do. They just tend to do it differently than women do.

Think about it. If a man wants to feel close to his buddies, does he call them up and ask to meet for lunch so they can talk? I think not. They do something together—play golf or tennis, go to a football game, hunt, fish. Men get close to other people through action rather than words. In fact, many men think that talking *ruins* intimate moments.

Your husband needs to feel connected to you, but for him, your *physical* relationship rather than your conversations is the tie that binds. Any form of physical contact—touching, kissing, petting, making love, having quickies—makes your husband feel closer to you. And once a man feels close to his wife "man style," he's more motivated to meet your need to talk and spend quality time together.

You don't have to have a degree in psychology to notice the unfortunate catch-22. Women need to feel satisfied emotionally in order to feel turned on or be motivated to satisfy their partners sexually. Men need to feel good about their sexual relationships in order to be invested in satisfying their wives emotionally. A go-nowhere waiting game is what happens next.

Sex-starved men wait for wives to become sexier, more flirtatious, and receptive to their sexual advances before putting energy into their relationships. They shut down emotionally. They end up watching inordinate amounts of television. They leave their soda cans in the family room. They forget they have children. They clam up.

This makes women feel communication starved. Communication-starved women feel depressed, short-changed, and resentful. They develop panic attacks, cry, overeat or undereat, lose sleep, take up residence in their less-than-attractive sweat suits, nag, criticize, and, last, but not least, shut the door on intimacy. The simply lose desire. When men tune out, women turn off. And when women turn off, men tune out.

Although you might be acutely aware of the ways in which your crabby, unresponsive, withdrawn husband zaps your desire, you might be less tuned in to the ways in which *your* lack of desire zaps *his* enthusiasm for your marriage and making you happy. If this sounds familiar to you, you may not like what I'm about to say, but you need to understand your role in this unfortunate cycle. You need to recognize how your actions are impeding any real closeness and connection with your husband and how a lack of closeness is making you feel unsexy.

When I tell women about this dilemma, they often say, "I cannot fathom how in the world my husband is interested in sex when we're not feeling close emotionally." If you've wondered about that, you probably have come to the following conclusion. You assume that your husband wants to be sexual because for him, having sex is like scratching an itch; it's a purely physical need. I wouldn't be surprised if you think this because many women do. But if you read nothing else in this book, please read the next few paragraphs. It may change your mind and save your marriage.

I'm convinced that one of the grossest misunderstandings about sex is the belief many women have that men desire sex because they just want or, better yet, need a physical release. It's true that men (and some women) love an occasional quickie without much emotional hoopla. However, I've been privileged to hear men describe the way they *really* feel when their wives aren't interested. And if you've assumed your husband wants sex just to "get off," what I've heard will undoubtedly surprise you.

When men talk about their sexual relationships with their wives, you can see strong emotion written on their faces. It's obviously an issue that touches something deep inside them. They start by telling me what a good physical relationship does for their hearts, minds, and souls. When they make love to their wives, they say they feel loved, accepted, appreciated, and cared for.

For me (a thirty-four-year-old male), sex = love. I need physical expressions of love to know that I am loved.

During lovemaking, men often give themselves permission to feel tender emotions that otherwise just lurk below the surface. Their wives' touches, kisses, and caresses trigger a feeling of connectedness and vulnerability that reinforces the love they feel for their partners.

I need to feel like she still finds me irresistible. Early in our marriage, if she wanted to make love, she would reach out and cuddle and start fondling and say "Hon," and her tender touches and kisses really heightened the experience for both of us. I felt her very being, the sexual energy oozing from her.

In addition to the closeness a man feels to his wife, a solid sexual relationship does wonders for his self-esteem and sense of masculinity. Little corrodes a man's feeling of confidence and sense of virility more than his wife's continual rejections.

My wife has started to refuse sex on a regular basis. We used to make love around four times per week, but now we do it once every two or three weeks. She recently told me that she isn't interested in sex at all, and hasn't been for four years or more.

I am so hurt that she doesn't want me. Now, I'm afraid to ask for sex for fear of rejection. Also, I'll never again be able to make love without wondering if she is only tolerating it.

I always have to initiate. When I get rejected it feels like a rejection of *me,* not of the activity. The rejection hurts.

Over time I've learned the hurt is best avoided by not initiating unless the chances of success are high enough. I only initiate now if:

1. It's a weekend night and not late.
2. The kids are in bed early or over at a friend's house for the night.
3. We've been getting along well that day.
4. It's the right half of the month (that's right, half).
5. I've had a couple of drinks so I forget the hurt, and she forgets she doesn't like me.

Since many men are raised to believe that their worth can be measured by their sexual prowess and their abilities to please their spouses sexually, men feel downright "unmanly" when sex is a trouble spot. They become depressed and feel shamed. Women often underestimate how important it is to so many men to satisfy their wives sexually. To men, sex is not just about receiving; it's about giving.

I wanted to please her in any way I could; her enjoyment came first and foremost. I was more turned on from pleasing her, and sometimes she didn't understand this. I had talked to her one night about wanting her to initiate it once in a while. I told her sometimes it makes me feel like she still loves me if she just touches me, fondles me, and maybe just kisses me. Her idea of initiating was this, "If you want any, you better get it before I fall asleep." I let her fall asleep. And then I would just lay there listening to her falling asleep and be so resentful. How could she feel love for me and not even try?

It's hard to believe that I've never had trouble pleasing a woman, but the one woman who matters, the one I love, the one I married, the one with whom I had my child, I can't please her. Makes me feel like a failure. She always told me not to worry, it wasn't my fault. It was *her* problem. What she never understood is that we are married . . . so her problems *are* my problems; that her feelings toward other things affect me as well.

One of the big reasons women with low desire don't fully understand or appreciate what their husbands experience is that men don't often share their feelings, especially feelings of insecurity, inadequacy, or vulnerability. They see it as a sign of weakness to let others in on these emotions. Rather than deal directly with their hurt, they become angry. And I don't have to tell you what a man's anger does to a woman's sexual desire. Anger is an amazingly effective desire buster. But you must remember this: if your husband has been angry, nasty, or unusually critical, it might just be a sign that he's crumbling inside.

Connie came to my office because her marriage was falling apart, and she wanted to give it one more try. She was ready to leave because her husband was angry all the time and nasty to her. Halfway through our session, I asked about her sex life, and she told me that they hadn't made love in years. Their five-year-old daughter had been sleeping with her since her birth—about the same time her husband had moved out. Not once had she questioned the obvious: that his anger might have had something to do with their separate bedrooms and lack of intimate connection. I felt certain that beneath his critical veneer, he simply missed his wife.

This is not to say that it's okay to be nasty. It isn't. If like Connie's husband, your spouse is angry, he will have to learn healthier, more productive ways to express his feelings. But in the meantime, despite his tough facade, you need to recognize that your husband really needs you and wants to be close to you both physically *and* emotionally—more than you'll ever know.

It took my husband sixteen years before he finally communicated the hurt and rejection in a way that I understood and I "got it." Before that, it was just the same old argument: he wanted more, I wanted less. He didn't seem to care that we had been arguing all day or I hadn't had two hours sleep with a sick kid or whatever. I could really take any problem and make it a reason to not want sex.

Granted, I had some very good reasons a lot of the time, but I also know sometimes I probably was punishing my husband for all the wrongs I felt he inflicted on me. I really didn't see sex as his way of expressing love for me. A lot of times I felt it didn't matter who was in the bed next to him; he just wanted some! Well, when I finally "got it," I did a complete 180, and actually really enjoyed it. I found my own sexuality again. My only regret is that I wish he had been able to talk to me in a way I could listen a long time ago. It could have prevented years of heartache.

If your spouse is stuck in the angry mode, let me do the talking for him. His anger is protective armor that shields his pain. Stop reacting to his ugly exterior, and look deeper into his soul. When you do, you can begin to chip away at the wall now separating you from your spouse and from your un-tapped sexual desire.

REAL MEN LIKE TO TALK TOO

As I told you earlier, many couples have a role reversal when it comes to the dynamic I just described. If you're the low-desire spouse and you're a man, you might feel exactly the same way women feel when their hus-bands withdraw emotionally or when they're hypercritical. You may lose desire for your wife.

I have worked with countless couples where this is so. Many men long for their wives' approval, appreciation, and recognition. Women's belief in their partners builds men's confidence, self-esteem, and sense of manli-ness. When, instead of support, men receive condemnation or ridicule or are nagged incessantly by their wives, they often cross their arms, put on their dark sunglasses, and check out emotionally. I've heard so many men tell their ranting and raving wives, "Whatever. You're always right. Just leave me alone." Emotional closeness and sexual intimacy become a thing of the past.

But one of the reasons these women give the appearance of wild women is that, like sex-starved men, they're desperately unhappy. They can't understand why their husbands don't want to touch them, make love to them, or be close physically. And in some ways, it's even harder for women when they're the more highly sexed spouse because almost every-one in the world assumes it's not supposed to be that way. Their husbands are supposed to chase them around the dining room table, remember? And when that doesn't happen, women have an especially hard time un-derstanding it and coping.

I know that many women aren't into sex like men, but my husband and I are quite the opposite. I remember in high school, my girl-friends and I were talking about how we would always be there to satisfy our husbands without them having to go elsewhere for grat-ification. Ha! If I don't ask for sex or make the first move, he can go for weeks without so much as a kiss.

Well, I've just celebrated four years of marriage, and I am starved for some good old-fashioned get-funky SEX. I know you're going to say talk to him. I have. It doesn't work. So I sit and plot how I will go out and have an affair just to have sex, and I will.

———————

I have a question for you: What if it is the *husband* who does not re-spond to sex at all? He has been to the doctor, who gave him a pre-scription for Viagra, but he will not use it. I have been living without sex for six years and don't know how much longer I can take it. He is a very nice guy, but I need sex too. I have tried everything to make him feel sexy, but to no avail. I am really angry, and I'm thinking of finding another man. I need it for survival, and to feel cared for. Sex is very important for both men and women.

*   *   *

If you've been feeling henpecked, misunderstood, nagged, or put down, I'm going to urge you to rise above your feelings of resentment and frus-tration. I'm going to push you to ask you to join the human race again and stop stonewalling your wife's genuine but misguided efforts to reach out to you. See her hurt and her longing. Understand that her self-esteem, pride, and sense of femininity has been under siege. Know that when she seems at her worst, she's at a loss for how to get through to you. Her temper tantrums, as unbecoming as they may be, signal the raw pain bubbling to the surface. She wants to connect with you, to touch you and to have you touch her. Reach inside and find not your defensiveness or apathy, but your compassion. Compassion is the conduit to connectedness.

As you can see, sexual desire is a complicated matter. You now know some of the questions to ask when it comes to rebuilding your passion for your spouse. In the next chapter, you'll learn about some of the solutions.

CHAPTER FOUR

Sexy Solutions

I want to give you a pat on the back for getting this far. It tells me that you're committed to boosting your desire and making your marriage more loving. You should feel great about that.

I have had many highly sexed spouses tell me that the problem in their marriages wasn't the differences in their sex drives as much as it was the fact that their partners were dismissive of their feelings and unwilling to do anything at all to address the issue. This created a tremendous sense of hurt. Here's an example of what more highly sexed spouses say.

The thing that I think makes a lack of sex a real threat to a marriage is the unwillingness of the low-desire partner to try to address the problem in any way, other than to expect the high-desire partner to grin and bear it. It hurts my feelings every time that my wife doesn't want to make love when I do, which is most days of my life. It makes me feel unloved, unattractive, unworthy, incompetent, etc. But it does not make me angry. What makes me angry is her unwilling-ness to do anything to make the situation better. I don't mean that I want her to just submit. I want her to search for behaviors that would bring more happiness to us both, to search for compromises, to try to express love more in other ways when she can't physically, to try to make our lovemaking especially good (instead in very plain vanilla) after I have patiently waited a long time for her to be ready, to read and discuss books that might help, to go to counseling, and even to being willing to discuss the problem in a loving way.

How can anyone not want to change, or at least lessen the impact of, behavior that he knows is causing his beloved spouse great unhappiness? (www.about.com/marriage)

So, you see, the fact that you're reading this tells me you're willing to explore new ways to improve things. That speaks volumes about your love for your spouse and your commitment to your marriage. I honor that in you. And your spouse will too. Regardless of what you do to improve your love life, as long as you do *something,* your spouse will appreciate your efforts. That, in and of itself, will begin to improve your relationship.

Don't assume that you must become an expert on low sexual desire before you intervene in some way. Although I think it's a great idea to become knowledgeable about what's happening within your body, your marriage, and your life, you shouldn't put off taking some action fairly soon. This chapter will point you to various starting places. Pick one, do something, and watch the results. If it helps, wonderful. If not, there are other approaches to explore. Boosting your desire isn't a precise science. What works for one person may not work for you. Just keep going until you find what works best for you and your spouse.

Since low desire is usually caused by a myriad of overlapping factors, don't waste time trying to figure out whether your low desire is due to one factor, such as a hormone imbalance, over another, such as your negative attitude toward your spouse, before trying something new. It might be both. And because it might be both, you can start by going to your doctor for a medical consultation or your friendly marital therapist to get to the bottom of your bad feelings, or taking a marriage seminar. Any of these actions might yield positive results.

In fact, you should also know that there is a reciprocal relationship between what you do, think, and feel and your body chemistry. Since your mind and body are inextricably interconnected, a change in your actions can alter your biochemistry, and a change in your body chemistry can alter how you think, feel, and act. For example, one of the best methods for treating a mild depression is exercise. Strenuous aerobic exercise stimulates, among other things, the release of endorphins, the body's natural opiate. The opposite is also true. For instance, take a couple who has argued for years about the wife's low sexual desire. And imagine what might happen when the wife finally agrees to take a testosterone supplement that stirs feelings of desire and excitement—something she hasn't felt for years. Think about the impact this might have on her, their sexual relationship, and their marriage in general. All of a sudden, the arguments stop, feelings of love reemerge, and they begin to reconnect emotionally. Clearly, there are many roads to a better sex life.

As you read through potential solutions in the biological, psychological, and relationship-oriented areas, you might notice that your relationship takes center stage. The reason for this is simple: I'm not a doctor; I'm not a psychologist; I'm a marital therapist. Marriages are my specialty. When professionals specialize in a certain area, they tend to see problems through that lens. This is not to say that biological or psychological solutions aren't useful or valid. They are. It's just that I will emphasize that which I know most about. If you feel convinced that the answer to your sexual difficulties lies in a biological solution such as taking Viagra, testosterone, or an anti-anxiety medication, then by all means, consult a physician and get a prescription. Trust your instincts.

With this in mind, as you read this chapter, make mental notes about the best place to begin your desire-boosting journey. And start there—today.

BIOLOGICAL SOLUTIONS

These are exciting times. A great deal is being learned about sexuality and the treatment of sexual problems. In fact, by the time this book is published, medical advances will have made available new cutting-edge medical treatments.

It certainly behooves you to visit your physician to eliminate all physiological causes for your drop in desire. You might discover simple solutions. For example, sometimes you can boost your desire simply by modifying medications you're taking. So step number one is to find a physician who is knowledgeable and comfortable talking to you about your sexuality. Not all are. Doctors don't necessarily receive human sexuality training in medical school. And even if they do, it doesn't mean that they are at ease discussing personal issues. Also, make certain your doctor takes you seriously and doesn't tell you that your concerns are just in your head. One of my clients had gone to her gynecologist complaining of low sexual desire. He asked, "Can you have orgasms?" and when she said she could, he replied, "Then it's all in your head. Don't worry about it." This "Don't worry, be happy" advice didn't work all that well.

You need to be an informed consumer and do your research before you go to your doctor. At the very least, you need to be able to describe your concern specifically. If you've noticed a drop in desire, don't just say, "I've lost my desire for sex." Give your doctor the details. For example, say, "For the last year, I have had no interest in initiating sex with my husband. Sometimes I have sex just to go along with him, but in the past, I was the one initiating two or three times a week." Or, "I don't feel like making love because it isn't enjoyable anymore. When my wife stimulates me, I don't become aroused. My penis doesn't become hard enough to have intercourse." Or, "When we start to have intercourse, I feel so dry that it hurts as my husband enters me, and I'm concerned about this." Get the picture?

If you've never spoken to anyone about your sexuality, having this sort of frank discussion won't be easy, but it's an important first step in getting the help you need, so push yourself to do it. And then make sure your doctor appears confident and competent in handling these issues. If not, you need to find another doctor. To do so, you can network through your friends if you are open enough to have discussed these issues. Getting a personal recommendation is often a good way to find a skilled professional. However, if talking with friends isn't something you do, especially about sexual matters, you might consider contacting a licensed sex therapist in your area and asking for a recommendation. At the end of this chapter, I offer you advice in seeking the assistance of a licensed sex therapist.

When it comes to feeling vibrant and sexual, nothing takes the place of being in good health. Take care of your body by eating healthfully, taking vitamins and antioxidants as needed, exercising (aerobic exercise tones muscles and increases blood flow to your entire body, and that includes your sex organs), getting enough sleep, drinking water, and caring for yourself psychologically and spiritually. No small order, but necessary nonetheless.

Other lifestyle choices can have a negative impact on your sex drive, such as smoking and drinking alcohol. If you've been overindulging, now is a good time to stop. And if stopping smoking has been a problem for you in the past, consider talking to your doctor about getting some help with Wellbutrin, which is often prescribed as a smoking-cessation aid and has the added benefit of boosting desire.

Testosterone

Many experts feel that one of the most promising biological treatments for desire problems is testosterone supplements. As you might recall, testosterone triggers sexual thoughts and fantasies and "puts you in the mood." Some people with low desire have abnormally low levels of testosterone.

People who take testosterone often report increased levels of desire and intensity of orgasms. Your doctor can do a full battery of blood tests to check your levels of free testosterone (the amount of testosterone in your body that is available to do the necessary work) and other important factors. Testosterone comes in many forms—pills, gels, ointments, patches, creams, injections, and lozenges.

If your doctor is unfamiliar with the tests required to assess your sexual functioning, you can refer him or her to Dr. Judith Reichman's book, *I'm Not in the Mood*. Dr. Reichman offers a concise list of the tests she recommends:

- Thyroid function (TSH, thyroid-stimulating hormone)
- Complete blood count to rule out anemia
- Prolactin level measurement
- Liver function
- Cholesterol and lipid profile
- DHEAS (dihydroepiandrosterone) levels
- FSH (follicle-stimulating hormone)

Like all other medications or hormone supplements, testosterone is not without the risk of undesirable side effects. Women taking even small doses of testosterone can experience virilizing effects, such as the growth of facial hair, a deepening of their voices, and problems with acne. You should not take testosterone if you are pregnant, have high cholesterol, a family history of heart disease, diabetes, hypertension, liver disease, acne, male pattern balding, or a history of breast cancer. It's extremely important to be under a physician's care while taking this hormone.

Medications

During a thorough medical checkup, your doctor will assess whether medications you're taking may be dampening your sexual desire. S/he may be able to offer you an alternative or consider lowering the dose. Here are some known culprits:

- Many antidepressants, tranquilizers, and mood stabilizers. Some antidepressants, such as Wellbutrin, do not lower desire.
- Some birth control pills.
- Hormone replacement therapy for women.
- Many other prescription and over-the-counter medications such as antacids, antibiotics, anti-epileptic medication, antihistamines, anti-inflammatories, and hypertension medications.
- Side effects of chemotherapy.

Discuss any and all medications you are currently taking, whether it is prescribed or over the counter.

Illness

Any life-threatening or significantly life-altering disease can dampen desire. Your doctor should have a complete medical history, including any chronic disease with which you are dealing. Sometimes when the illness causing the drop in desire is addressed, sexual problems become resolved. For example, if you are clinically depressed, it's a pretty safe assumption that you're not going to be all that interested in sex. When you begin to take steps to deal with your depression, your sexual energy may return as well. However, it is also the case that certain medications used to treat diseases also dampen desire. Again, your doctor can offer you substitutions or consider changing the dose. As a reminder, the following is a partial list of diseases known to have desire-lowering effect:

Heart and lung disease	Rheumatoid arthritis
Liver, kidney, and pituitary disease	Cancer
Anemia	Thyroid disease
Parkinson's disease	High blood pressure
Diabetes	Lupus

Sexual Problems

If your drop in desire is due to other sexual problems mentioned in the previous chapter, here are some options to consider. Keep in mind that the following sexual difficulties can have several causal factors.

DYSPAREUNIA

If you're experiencing pain during intercourse, that is, dyspareunia, it may be due to the fact that you aren't lubricating enough. Rubbing dry skin against dry skin doesn't feel very good. Your doctor might recommend taking hormones such as estrogen or progesterone. Estrogen comes in many forms—a pill, patch, vaginal rings (inserted like a diaphragm), and topical cream. If you prefer not to take hormones, good old-fashioned lubricants such as K-Y Jelly and similar products can help.

If you are experiencing pain when your spouse penetrates you, it may be due to vaginismus—the involuntary spasming of parts of your vagina. If this is happening to you, you can be taught techniques to relax. A sex therapist can offer you a great deal of help with this. Vaginal infections are another cause for pain during intercourse. Following a proper diagnosis, infections can be treated effectively with antibiotics.

AROUSAL PROBLEMS IN WOMEN

Arousal problems are often caused by inadequate blood flow to the vagina, labia, and clitoris, which prevents engorgement or swelling, increased sensation, and lubrication. There are many reasons this can happen, including hysterectomy and other pelvic surgeries that injure nerves and blood vessels.

Several methods are being used to overcome arousal problems. Viagra (sildenafil) holds promise for women as a means of increasing blood flow to the genital area. It is currently being researched for approval by the Food and Drug Administration. Another treatment for inadequate blood flow is the Eros-CTD (clitoral therapy device), a small pump with a cup-like attachment that women place over their clitoris and surrounding tissue. The pump simulates oral sex and increases blood flow. In addition to feeling pleasurable, the suction created by the pump is believed to prevent collagen deposits that build up in the arteries leading to the clitoris.

ERECTILE DYSFUNCTION

If your interest in sex has vanished because you are having difficulties getting or keeping an erection, you should definitely speak with your doctor. Erectile dysfunction is often due to physiological causes, such as heart disease, hypertension, high cholesterol, diabetes, vascular disease and injuries, surgical procedures including prostate cancer surgery, smoking, medications, and alcohol use.

The good news is that erectile dysfunction is treatable. One very popular line of treatment is Viagra, (sildenafil), which increases blood flow to the penis and in most men creates the ability to have an erection within an hour. For many couples, this drug has been a blessing. For others, it has created new and unintended problems. Regaining erectile function within an hour after struggling for months or years changes relationship dynamics faster than the speed of light. For this and other reasons, if you are interested in taking Viagra, most experts agree that it's best to combine it with sex or marital therapy.

Uprima (apomorphine) is a newer solution for erectile dysfunction. Uprima tablets are dissolved under the tongue and produce erections in men in less time than Viagra. However, as of the writing of this book, it has not yet been approved for sale in the United States.

More invasive but effective methods such as penile injections or implants are also available.

If you have prostate cancer and you require surgery, seek a skilled doctor who is knowledgeable about performing nerve-sparing surgery to prevent erectile difficulties.

Beyond medication and sex therapy, sex education has proven effective to reduce or eliminate erectile problems.

PREMATURE OR EARLY EJACULATION

If you're a man whose desire has plummeted because you ejaculate before intercourse, shortly after penetration, or before your spouse is satisfied, there's hope for you. Early ejaculation is the most common sexual complaint among men. Therapy that provides support and information and facilitates communication between you and your spouse has proven effective. You can also learn specific skills to help you relax and gain control over your ejaculations. Some antidepressants known to dull arousal, such as Zoloft and Prozac, are being used to treat early ejaculation too.

RESOLVING PSYCHOLOGICAL ISSUES

In Chapter 2, I described a number of personal issues that are sure to deaden your interest in sex. Now I want to give you some tools to help you begin to break through the mental stumbling blocks that have been keeping you at arm's length from a better sexual relationship.

No matter why you're feeling unhappy—you're bored to death with your job, you hate looking in the mirror because of the extra twenty pounds, you're stressed to the max, or you've got a bad case of free-floating anxiety—you need to decide that it's time to do something to help yourself feel better. *You* are responsible for changing the way you feel. If you are miserable, no amount of wishing and hoping and planning and thinking will change things. *You have to take action.* You, and you alone, have to decide that your less-than-vibrant mental health has been deadening your passion, and it's time for a change. Don't hide behind your bad feelings as a way of avoiding dealing with tough issues. Face these issues head-on.

First, know that things probably aren't as bleak as you think. People who are down in the dumps tend to look at things in ways that makes matters worse. When they reflect on their lives, they have what is referred to as selective perception, that is, they tend to recall only the negative.

Conversely, people who are in good spirits tend to emphasize more of the positives when reflecting on their experiences in the past. Our current mood acts as a lens that dictates what we recall and what we forget.

There's another thing about people who feel down and out: they tell themselves that they'll feel the same way tomorrow . . . and the day after that and the day after that. This sort of pessimistic thinking gets them in trouble because it continues to make them feel lousy. And if you continue to feel lousy, you won't feel inspired to take action.

But here's an alternative. Even if you're not in the mood, get your feet moving. Make a commitment to change your life, no matter what mood you're in. Do it for you. Do it for your marriage. Do it for your children if you have them. You're not good for anyone if you're unhappy with yourself. I'm going to get you started, but you will need to continue to expand on the steps you've taken here. I suggest that you read my book *Change Your Life and Everyone in It* for a more complete program for change.

Setting Goals

The first step to making yourself happier is to figure out specifically what you want to change. You need a goal. And if you think you already know what you want to change, think again. I can tell you without even knowing you that your goals are probably half-baked, and you need to work on them a bit more. I know this because most people's goals are far too vague to be helpful.

For starters, I'd like for you to write your goals down on paper, an important first step. Once you commit your goals to paper, you can document your progress. When you get further down the road, you can look back and see how far you've come. Written goals are a strong indication that you're taking yourself seriously. Plus, committing your goals to writing is an action. This can be the first of many productive actions you're about to take. In a moment, I would like for you to respond to the question, "What are two or three things I want to change or improve about myself or my life?" But before you do, read the following three criteria for developing solution-oriented goals. When your goals take the three criteria into account, they will contain seeds for solutions.

1. Describe what you want to change about your life rather than what you're unhappy about.

When I ask people, "What are you hoping to change about your life?" they generally don't answer my question. Instead, they tell me why they're miserable. For example, they'll say, "I just hate my body," or "I'm depressed." These comments are complaints, not goals. They tell me a little about why people are unhappy, but nothing about what people want to have happen instead. As long as you focus on why you're unhappy, you won't get very far. Here's how to fix that.

If you feel depressed, ask yourself, "When I start feeling a bit better, what will I be doing differently?" You might respond, "I will like myself more," or "I will be more energetic." Similarly, if your body image is a problem, ask yourself, "When I start feeling better about my body, what will I be doing differently?" Perhaps your response might be, "I will accept myself the way I am," or "I will decide to do something positive about my weight." Those are better responses. They're not quite solution oriented, but they're a step in the right direction because they point to what will be happening when the problem is solved.

2. Describe your goals in action-oriented terms.

The second solution-oriented goal-setting criterion is that your response must be in behavioral terms. If I were a fly on the wall in your home and you were achieving your goal, what would I actually see you doing? Let's go back to the example of someone who is unhappy with her body. She said, "I will feel better about my body." Although this addresses what she wants rather than what she is unhappy about, it is not an action-oriented statement and therefore is not specific enough. It's about a feeling, not a behavior. To transform it into an action-oriented statement, she should ask herself, "When I'm feeling better about my body, what exactly will I be *doing* that I'm not doing now?" If her answer is, "I will begin a new regimen of exercising for a half-hour four times a week," then she has hit the action-oriented mark. That's good.

Similarly, if you believe you will be more energetic and start liking yourself when you start to feel less depressed, you need to ask yourself what specifically you will be doing that will clue you in that you're energetic and more self-accepting. Your response might be, "I will get up every morning, take a shower, and go for a walk," or "I will be able to think about myself and my accomplishments and say to myself, 'I've done good things with my life.' "

Another helpful question to ask yourself is, "How, will my spouse, children, friends, colleagues know when I'm_____[less stressed out, more relaxed, and so on]? What will they see me *doing* that will clue them in that my life has taken a turn for the better?" You might respond, "My spouse will see me joke around with him or initiate more conversation, play the piano again, or read in the evenings" or "My kids will start to see me smiling more and being more patient with them instead of yelling."

3. Make sure your goals are broken down into small, do-able steps.

Often, people are unable to reach their goals because they are too grandiose or unachievable in a reasonable time period. If the goals you set are too big, you will feel frustrated because you won't see very much progress. Research has taught us that the best way to motivate people to keep on track of their goals is for them to recognize the small steps forward. When you notice that you are making progress, it is incredibly reinforcing; you want to keep going.

Let's go back to the example of the woman who wants to feel better about her body. She told us that when she starts working out four times a week, she'll be on her way to feeling better. But there is still a problem with her goal. Few people go from being sedentary to working out a half-hour four times a week regularly. That would be like accelerating from zero to eighty-five miles per hour in two seconds flat. It just doesn't happen that way.

Instead, she should ask herself, "What will be *the very first sign* that I'm moving in the right direction?" If she answers, "I will buy some workout clothes and join the health club a mile from my home this week," then she's cooking. Once she accomplishes this milestone, she might add, "I will work out for at least fifteen minutes two or three times a week," gradually working her way up to her ultimate goal. Your goals should be accomplishable within a week or two. If they're not, break them down into smaller steps.

Now let's look at an example of how a person was able to improve her frame of mind and, as a result, her sexual relationship by identifying concrete, action-oriented and do-able goals. Meet Carrie.

Carrie's marriage was in trouble when she and I first met. Her husband had informed her that he didn't plan on continuing to live "like brother and sister" anymore, and that he was considering leaving their marriage if things didn't change. I started by asking Carrie if she knew what he meant when he said "brother and sister," and she said, "Rich and I have talked about this a lot. We only make love once or twice a month, and I know that's not enough for him. He'd prefer if we made love at least once a week and, when we did, if I were more into it. I want him to be happy. I just don't know where to begin."

I began by asking Carrie whether she enjoyed being sexual with Rich, and she said, "Once we start making love, I enjoy it, but when he initiates sex, I often turn him down because I'm thinking of everything else that I have to do." Carrie went on to say, "I'm always so frazzled and preoccupied. I'm really disorganized. Each day goes by without my accomplishing half of what I had hoped to do. I feel totally stressed out, and I don't feel like making love."

I wanted to know whether Carrie's disinterest in sex was related to underlying resentment about her work load at home, and so I asked whether Rich helped her with the responsibilities, and she promptly said, "Absolutely. He's a great partner. I have no complaints about that."

"Carrie," I asked, "what would have to happen for you to feel less stressed all the time?" She replied, "I've thought about this idea, but I've never done it before. I imagine that if I were to make to-do lists every day and cross items off when I accomplished them, I would get more done. That way, I would have more time in the evening to devote to family and, in particular, Rich. I could start there." That sounded like a positive, action-oriented first step. "Anything else?" I wondered, and she said, "Yes. "It would also help if we could get the kids to bed a little earlier so that we can have some private time in the evening. Rich would be willing to help with that. I'd just have to ask."

She had one more idea. Carrie often felt stressed about the possibility that the children would walk into their bedroom while they were being intimate, and this made her feel like avoiding sex. She realized that it might help her to relax if Rich put a lock on their bedroom door. Although she had thought about this solution before, she never asked Rich to do it. Carrie felt convinced that not only would Rich be happy to install a lock, but that he would see this request as a sign that she was taking his issues about their sex life seriously.

I said to Carrie, "In addition to feeling less stressed so that you're more available to Rich sexually, you mentioned that he would like it if you were more into it. What would you have to do in order for him to feel you were more excited?" She replied, "He says he wants me to kiss him more, talk to him, and make more noise while we're making love."

The interesting point about Carrie's situation is that prior to our setting goals and discussing the action-oriented, do-able steps she could take to feel more at ease with herself, a better sexual relationship seemed out of reach. Once she could imagine how she could feel more relaxed by making minor shifts in her daily routine and in her lovemaking, she felt infinitely more optimistic about making real changes in her marriage.

*   *   *

Now that you have learned about the three important goal-setting criteria, it's time for you to set your personal goals. When you answer the question, "What are you hoping to change about yourself or your life?" it's best to limit your response to no more than three items. You don't want to feel overwhelmed. It's best to start small. Good things come in small packages. So, write your goals now.

Once you've identified your goals, you should have a pretty good idea about one or two things that you can do immediately to get yourself on track. Taking one small step won't resolve all the things that are troubling you, but you will feel a tremendous sense of relief knowing that you are doing something to improve your outlook and mental health. Besides, it's important for you to remember that a journey of a thousand miles begins with one small step forward. So, take that small step.

Once you begin the process of change, it helps to keep track of your progress. You can do this by asking yourself the following questions:

> On a 1 to 10 scale, with 10 being the best I've ever felt and 1 being the worst, how would I have rated things when I hit my lowest point?

How do I rate things now?

Where on the scale do I need to be in order to feel satisfied?

Let's say that at your lowest point, you were at a 2. Then, after doing a few things to improve your life, you estimate that you are at a 6 but that you'd like to be at an 8 in order to feel satisfied. Here's the next question to ask:

"What would be one or two things I could do in the next week or two that would bring me up from a 6 to a 6 1/2 or 7?

Remember, your answers should always be action oriented.

Sometimes when you've been struggling with issues for a long time, it's difficult to get out of your rut by yourself. You may need some help. If you aren't reaching out to supportive friends and family, you should do so immediately. We all need a little help from our friends from time to time. Don't use the excuse that they're too busy or they don't care about you. Chances are that if they knew you were having a rough time, they would be happy to do whatever they could. It's challenging to solve problems when you isolate yourself from people who love you.

If you are too far from loved ones or for a variety of reasons prefer not to talk to them, consider seeking the help of a trained professional. As I said before, the best way to find a good therapist is word of mouth. Satisfied customers offer invaluable information about the quality of therapy you will receive.

Make sure your therapist has received specific training and is experienced in dealing with your particular concern. You might consider interviewing your therapist over the phone to ask about his or her level of experience. Don't be shy about it. You should feel comfortable and respected by your therapist. You should feel that he or she understands your perspective and feelings. If you aren't comfortable with something your therapist is suggesting, say so. If your therapist honors your feedback, that's a good sign. If not, leave.

Make sure you and your therapist set concrete goals early on. If you don't, you will probably meet each week with no clear direction. Once you set goals, keep them in plain view. If you don't begin to see some progress within a few sessions, discuss this with your therapist.

Many therapists believe that it's important to understand the impact of your upbringing on who you are as an adult before finding solutions to your current problems. Sometimes this is helpful, but unless you shift gears and start to discuss what you can do about your situation, you will get stuck in the past. There's no question that putting the puzzle pieces together can be interesting and insight producing, but insight doesn't lead to change. Insight leads to insight. Change leads to change.

Seek a therapist who has a future orientation—one who will ask, "Where do you want to be a week, month, year from now?" and who will help you figure out the specific steps you need to take to get there. If the therapist you choose doesn't do that, you should redirect him or her. If s/he isn't willing to take your lead, find a therapist who will.

If, when you go to a therapist, you think you might end up discussing not only the personal issues with which you are concerned but also your marriage, it is of utmost importance that you find a therapist who believes in the sanctity of marriage. Too many therapists inadvertently help people out of their marriages, especially if you start out going by yourself. If you go to a therapist without your spouse and the therapist isn't committed to helping people keep their marriages intact, once you start complaining about your spouse and the troubles in your marriage, it's possible that your therapist will start asking questions like, "Do you really love your spouse?" "Why would you put up with that?" "Don't you think the kids would be better off if you were separated?" "Why do you think you married such a controlling person?" "Don't you think you'd be happier on your own?" By the time you're done with the session, you will start doubting your commitment to your marriage.

It's unfortunate, but there aren't enough therapists who understand that marriages, even the best of marriages, involve hard work and have incredible ups and downs. People who understand this about relationships and are willing to do what it takes to work through the rough spots and weather the storm benefit greatly. Most people who stick it out through the hard times are very, very happy they did.

If, in addition to the personal issues this section addresses, you are struggling with relationship issues, besides reading the section that follows, get some help for your marriage. Make sure you ask your therapist his or her views of divorce. You can even ask what percentage of the time couples in the therapist's practice leave with their marriages intact. Your therapist probably won't be able to answer specifically because few track these data, but the response will be very telling nonetheless. If your marriage is part of what is making you unhappy, unless there is domestic violence or serious problems such as chronic substance abuse, learning relationship skills is the answer, not leaving.

Most of all, trust your instincts. If your therapist is helping, you'll know it. If s/he isn't, you'll know that too. Don't stay with a therapist just because s/he is nice. Find one who is nice and helpful.

Sex Drive Zappers

In a moment, I am going to offer some relationship-oriented solutions. But before we switch gears, I have a few more thoughts to share with you about some of the most common personal issues that can zap a person's sex drive.

NOW I'M A MOM, NOT A SEXUAL BEING

Many women say that once their children are born, they start thinking of themselves more as mothers and less as sexual beings. Their once-toned bodies often lose shape. Their milk-producing breasts became vessels of nourishment, not objects of sensual delight. The constant physical contact involved with the care of infants and young children triggers a tactile overload in some women, making their husbands' touch undersirable. Their belief that they turn fewer heads pushing baby carriages down the street than they did in their pre-mommy days leaves them grieving the loss of their more attractive and sensual selves.

If you're a woman to whom all this sounds familiar, it's important for you to know how common these feelings really are. Childbirth brings with it tremendous change. And no matter how much you wanted to have children and bless the day they arrived, nothing prepares you for the ways in which your life has been transformed. It makes perfect sense that you're reevaluating who you are and what the future holds for you.

But it's also important to keep in mind that eventually you will start to feel more comfortable with your new identity and role as mother. You have a very important new job, and it's not surprising that you're taking it to heart. However, one of the biggest mistakes I see women make in their marriages is that once the children are born, they forget they have husbands.

Busy with their new responsibilities, women believe that their husbands are independent and therefore should just take care of themselves. Women stop paying attention. They stop nurturing and stop being affectionate to the men they love. They quit packing box lunches, calling just to say hi, planning a date night out, or being up for a spontaneous late-night tryst. They resign as wives and enlist as full-time mothers. And contrary to what women believe, this abrupt withdrawal of attention and connection crushes men. They feel abandoned. They even feel jealous of that little person who stole their wives' heart. If men protest—and they often do—women think them selfish and immerse themselves more completely in their mothering duties.

If you've stopped feeling sexual because of being bitten by the motherhood bug, it's important to make a conscious decision to make your marriage a priority. I always say that the best thing you can do for your children is to put your marriage first. Take more time for your spouse. Get a babysitter—a family member or close friend—and go out. Don't neglect your husband. The more he feels important in your life, the closer you'll be, and the more connected he'll feel to you and your children. And if you're like most other women, this strong emotional bond can be an aphrodisiac.

I HATE MY BODY

If you dislike your body, you're in good company. Countless people feel exactly the same way. But when you consider how many people are dissatisfied with their bodies, one would expect their spouses to be complaining in equal numbers. But they're not. Yes, some people want their spouses to be trimmer, more muscular, shapelier, more buff or more buxom, but more often than not, you are your own worst critic.

If you are hard on yourself, it's time to begin the journey to self-acceptance. Focus on your good points. Find ways to flaunt them, and learn how to accept the rest. Take a moment to imagine how different your life would be if you truly stopped worrying about your imperfections once and for all. Envision how freeing that would be. No matter how long you've been feeling badly about yourself, you can make a decision that will change your life forever. You can decide to stop striving to be a Victoria's Secret model or Arnold Schwarzenegger lookalike and just be yourself.

Andrea and Rich, a couple in their early fifties, were concerned that their marriage of ten years had become stale. Although they saw themselves as having a good relationship in general, they were noticing early signs of discontent and disconnection. During the evenings after work, they usually busied themselves with solitary activities and spoke infrequently. They socialized on the weekends with friends but almost never spent time alone. Since this was a second marriage for both of them, they understood the challenges of divorce and were determined to nip their relationship problems in the bud.

Halfway through the session, Andrea mentioned that she would like more time with Rich in the evening. But when asked what she would like to be doing, Andrea said, "In reality, I guess I don't have much energy after work. Although I think I want to spend more time with Rich, in truth, I'm glad he's leaving me alone."

Over the years, I have learned that couples often use cryptic language when it comes to sex, and I couldn't help but wonder whether Andrea's "fatigue" and wanting to be left alone had something to do with a waning sexual desire. So I asked her, "How's your sex life?" As she shared her thoughts, it became clear that I hit the nail on the head.

For several years, Andrea had had no sexual appetite whatsoever. She recalled times in their marriage when she desired Rich, but those days were long gone. There were some obvious red flags: a hysterectomy, menopause, and medication for her underfunctioning thyroid, all warranting further investigation. Above and beyond the biological factors was a personal issue that, when it came to lovemaking, stopped Andrea dead in her tracks: her feelings about her body. In the last few years, Andrea, like many other women her age, had put on some weight. One could see the pain on Andrea's face when she told me that she didn't think she was attractive anymore. She assumed her husband felt the same way. Although Rich denied feeling less attracted to Andrea because of her weight gain, she thought he was being dishonest, and nothing he said to the contrary reassured her. Although initially, I tried to help Rich explain that he was still completely attracted to Andrea, it wasn't working at all. The problem was that Andrea had stopped feeling attracted to Andrea.

Rather than debate with Andrea about her self-image, I said, "Okay, fine. So what are you going to do to feel better about yourself?" and she said, "I'm going to start working out at the gym three or four times a week." I responded, "That sounds great. When do you start?" She said, "I always tell myself that I'm going to go back to the gym, but I never do." I thanked her for her honesty and suggested she come up with a completely different, perhaps less ambitious, starting place. After some thought, she said, "I'd really like it if Rich would agree to walk with me every evening. That would be a good start." Rich, wanting to get back into an exercise program himself, was happy to oblige.

When they returned three weeks later, I discovered that the walking had paid off. It's not that Andrea lost so much weight or that she had firmed up her body, but the fact that she had done what she had set out to do vastly improved her outlook, plus Andrea and Rich found that their evening walks invited more intimate conversation. Andrea's increased optimism and sense of closeness to Rich boosted her desire to be with him sexually. Their holding hands throughout the session was a dead giveaway.

If you're miserable about your body, figure out what's changeable and what isn't. Set new getting-in-shape goals based on the goal-setting section in this chapter. Then start to work in earnest on the parts of your body that are modifiable. After that, memorize and live by the popular serenity prayer:

> God, grant me the serenity to accept the things I cannot change, the courage to change the things I can, and the wisdom to know the difference.

A twist on the "I hate my body" theme is "I'm not interested in sex because I am not attracted to my spouse." If your spouse has stopped putting effort into staying in shape and good health, it might be a turn-off to you. Let's face it: physical attraction is very important.

If your spouse's health habits aren't what they should be, I will address this issue with him or her later in this book. I will discuss the importance of physical attraction and being in good health when it comes to having a vibrant sex life. I might be able to get through to him or her even though you haven't. Sometimes it helps to have an outside source saying the same thing you've been saying.

In the meantime, here are some things you should consider. No matter what physical changes your spouse needs to make for you to feel attraction again, it's going to take time for those changes to occur. You can't lose twenty pounds or build muscle overnight. If you wait until s/he reaches his or her goal, your marriage may fall apart. When you see your partner making an effort to get in shape or lead a more healthful lifestyle, you can encourage him or her to stick to the plan by complimenting those efforts and even being affectionate. That will go a long way to increasing your spouse's stick-to-itiveness.

If you're saying to yourself, "Ah yes, but we've been down this road before; s/he never sticks to his or her resolution," that attitude must go. Research tells us that people who make substantial changes in their lives—lose weight, stop smoking and/or drinking—have many setbacks before they make a healthier lifestyle a way of life (Prochaska, Norcross, and DiClemente, 1994). Stop being critical and pessimistic. Support your spouse's efforts to change. If you start being more physically affectionate, you will give your partner's ego the boost it needs to keep the positive changes going.

BUT I'VE HAD BAD EXPERIENCES IN THE PAST

Sometimes what's holding you back from having a better sexual relationship with your spouse are painful memories of past physical, sexual, or emotional abuse. Traumatic experiences can trigger bad feelings that have a lasting effect. Some people aren't even aware of the extent to which negative experiences have scarred them emotionally. They fear intimacy. They don't enjoy being touched. They have a hard time letting their guard down and relaxing with their partners. They experience flashbacks.

It is important for you to know that sexual, physical, and emotional abuse is very common, as are feelings of shame, guilt, anxiety, and anger. But these feelings don't have to hold you prisoner of the past. You can and should do something about them. You should seek professional help. You might be feeling ashamed to talk to anyone about what happened in your life, but you shouldn't allow your shame to hold you back. Trained therapists are able to help you overcome unresolved feelings that might be preventing you from leading a rich and satisfying life.

But I don't want you to assume that if you're not really into sex, something must have happened to you as a child. As you now know, there are an infinite number of reasons you can be experiencing low sexual desire that have absolutely nothing to do with a troubled past. In fact, even if you were unfortunate enough to have experienced sexual abuse—unwanted fondling or even rape—don't immediately assume your low desire is due to that experience. It may or may not be. Let me give you a couple of examples.

I knew a woman who was a jogger. One day she went out for her run and returned to her apartment to find a man hiding behind the door, wearing a ski mask and holding a knife. She told herself, "I'll let him rape me if that's what he's after, but I'm going to get out of this alive." He had her take her clothes off and then raped her. Within moments, he had an orgasm, and she saw an opportunity to flee. She ran to a neighbor, who offered her clothes and a phone to call the police. When the police arrived, they grilled her about the rape. She very matter-of-factly described what had happened. Confused, the policeman said to the woman, "I don't get it. You were just raped at knifepoint, and you're sitting here, calmly, telling me the details. How can you be so calm?" and without hesitation she responded, "You don't think that I'm going to let ten minutes with that f**ker ruin my life, do you?"

I remember my response when I heard that story. I felt like shouting *Yes!!!!* I loved her resilience and strength. I loved that she refused to allow herself to become a psychological victim. Her story of resilience has left an imprint in my head and in my heart, and it's something I often share with others. This woman went on to do work with rape victims, helping them move forward in their lives. She is also married, has children, and enjoys a healthy and satisfying sex life. She doesn't see herself as damaged goods. She taught me a very important lesson: that the most important thing in life is not what happens but the meaning we ascribe to what happens—the stories we tell ourselves about our experiences.

Here's another example. I worked with Connie and Phil, a couple in their forties with three children. Phil felt that their sex life was a low priority to Connie. A stay-at-home mom, Connie was extremely active in their children's schools, with volunteer work, church-related activities, and her friends. When it came to Phil, she had nothing left to give.

I worked with them for several sessions before Phil said, "Connie, don't you think you ought to tell Michele what happened to you?" Connie replied, "I suppose," and proceeded to tell me that when she was young, a cousin molested her repeatedly. But then added, "I don't think this has anything to do with why I'm not too sexual," and quickly turned to me and asked, "Do you?"

Before answering her question, I wanted to know if she enjoys sex and is orgasmic, and the answer to both questions was yes. Then she said, "I rarely think about what happened as a child. I never have flashbacks. I strongly believe that what happened, happened. It's over, and there's nothing I can do about it. I don't relive the memories at all."

I needed no further convincing. I told her that it was entirely possible that she had really come to terms with the past and that her current lack of interest in sex was completely unrelated to that experience. We discussed some specific things she could change about the way she structured her day that would send the message to her husband that he was important to her. I suggested that Phil look for signs that Connie was truly at peace with her past. They returned two weeks later, smiling. Apparently, they had had considerably more sex, and both of them appeared genuinely happy, so much so that they were planning a weekend getaway. Several months later, the fire was still burning.

Connie just needed a little reassurance that she had actually put the past to rest and that her lack of interest in sex was not a sign she still had more emotional work to do. It is so important that you not label yourself as "damaged goods" because of past abusive situations that I want to give you one more example.

I worked with a bright, energetic man in his thirties named Sol. He and his wife had been married for ten years, and they had two children. When Sol came to my office, he told me that their sex life had been suffering because of performance anxiety. When they would begin to make love, he would get so tense that he often lost his erection. He felt overwhelmed by his frustration and fear that he would spend the rest of his life experiencing sexual failure.

I asked Sol what he had tried thus far to feel more comfort when he and his wife were intimate. Sol proceeded to share with me a long list of treatment failures. He started by seeking help from a therapist who, when she heard about his punitive, alcoholic parents and a molestation in his youth, convinced him that he had emotional baggage that needing working through. She spent many sessions encouraging him to remember the most painful times in his life. When I asked whether he found the time with her helpful, he replied, "It made things worse. I always knew my childhood was painful. But after working with that therapist, I *became* my painful past. She believed that my anxiety was the direct result of my childhood experiences, and I became damaged goods. It was really depressing." So I asked, "What did you do next?"

He told me that he attended a nationally renowned sex clinic where they provided education about erectile dysfunction and offered new ways to look at his sexual difficulties with his wife. "They didn't discuss my childhood, but they told me that I must have issues with my wife. Although I thought my marriage was on fairly stable ground, I started to explore reasons that I might be angry with her. The only thing I could think of was that she wasn't particularly experimental in bed. Once I honed in on that and criticized her, I found myself getting angrier and angrier, and our sex life deteriorated even more. Eventually, I stopped searching for plausible resentments and said to myself, 'My wife wants to have sex several times a week, and that's a heck of a lot more than most guys can say.' I felt better about her, but I still was at a loss about my sexual difficulties."

As Sol spoke, what struck me was the incredible determination this man had for finding solutions, for being close to his wife, for not giving up, even in the face of possible failure and paralyzing anxiety and unhelpful advice. I was in awe of his perseverance and the internal strength required to reject professional diagnoses that he intuitively knew would hurt rather than help him grow.

Aware of his turbulent past, I said, "I know your parents were harsh and punitive, but you just have to tell me where in the world your resilience and stick-to-it-iveness comes from. There must have been someone in your past who believed in you. Who might that have been?" After minutes of silence that seemed like years, Sol tearfully responded, "My grandmother loved me. She was very affectionate. She never yelled at me. She didn't have to. My grandmother never uttered an unkind word. She just hugged and kissed me." Again, a long silence. "I guess my grandfather believed in me too. He was a man of few words, but when he spoke, he let me know that I was okay. I recall that his words of support were confusing because at the time, I was always getting so many negative messages from my parents. But my grandfather loved me unconditionally."

As Sol spoke about his grandparents, I could see his expression change. He sat up in his chair. The tears stopped. Memories of his grandparents lit his face with smiles. And he gradually began to talk about his strength in coping with his childhood, in overcoming his fears, in being successful as a man, father, and husband. And finally, I got the full picture of his sexual relationship with his wife.

Although he struggled to maintain his erections from time to time, it was by no means a pervasive problem. In fact, despite some rocky starts, he more often than not managed to maintain an erection long enough for both he and his wife to experience orgasms. He didn't share his successes with past therapists because when he mentioned them casually, they seemed disinterested in these "flukes." They were more interested in the problem—his anxiety and the times his penis became flaccid—and as a result, so was he—so much so that he had become obsessed with it.

But our conversation was a turning point for Sol. My fascination with his strength and resilience made him more curious about those parts of himself, and as he began to think of himself not as damaged goods but as a person who rose above adversity, his sexual confidence increased as well. I saw Sol and his wife for several more sessions, and their marriage was blooming.

This is not to say that Sol never had difficulties with erections again. He did. But I helped him and his wife to understand setbacks are incredibly common. They just had to figure out what they needed to do to get things back on track and then do it without getting frustrated or upset. And that's what they did. For that matter, that's what they're probably still doing.

If you've had traumatic experiences, the important thing for you to remember is that you do not have to allow those experiences to define you.

If you are having trouble leaving the past in the past, don't waste another day thinking about it. Go get some help. And as with Sol, if your initial attempts at getting help aren't effective, don't give up.

RELATIONSHIP SOLUTIONS: MARRIAGE WOULD BE EASY IF IT WEREN'T FOR YOU . . .

In the previous chapter, I explored why spouses often feel angry, disappointed, resentful, and distant from one another. I also explained how these negative feelings can keep you at an arm's length from a better sexual relationship with your spouse. If you're harboring any of these unpleasant feelings, you need to do something about them. Unless you find solutions to your marital problems, your sex drive will stay stuck in neutral.

If, for example, you feel that your husband always stands up for his family rather than you when there is a family conflict, your hurt might prompt you to avoid intimacy altogether. You've got to work out a better understanding between the two of you if you are ever to feel close enough to him to desire him. If your wife's spending habits infuriate you but she refuses to acknowledge your feelings or be more prudent with money, your resentment might make you shut down emotionally. If you don't find a solution to your divergent spending habits, your frustration might ruin any closeness you once felt and rob you of desire.

To help you find some solutions to your ongoing relationship issues, I will share with you several relationship skeleton keys—problem-solving formulas that you can apply to most relationship difficulties. Once you stop fighting, clear the air, and start getting along better, you'll feel a sense of closeness that will begin to bridge the desire gap. In addition, I will also give you a number of suggestions designed to deal more specifically with the gap in your desire levels. By working on both your relationship and sexual issues at the same time, you will be armed with a powerful two-prong approach.

Before you head straight for the solutions, I want to remind you about the importance of knowing exactly what it is that you're hoping to change about your marriage and sex drive. Review the goal-setting section in this chapter. You need to familiarize yourself with solution-oriented goal-setting principles so that you can apply these principles to setting relationship goals. Begin your journey to an improved marriage and sexual relationship by asking yourself:

What am I hoping to change about my marriage?
How will I know that things are moving in the right direction?
What will be the first sign that my sex drive is getting on track?
What will my spouse notice about me when my passion returns?

Now, set your relationship goals.

Here's an example of a couple who was able to make significant progress in improving their sexual relationship once they became clearer about what they actually wanted from each other.

Brent and Catherine were at odds about their sexual relationship. Brent liked making love early in the morning, every morning, and Catherine preferred evening hours but certainly not every evening. Brent jokingly said, "With Catherine, there is a one-hour window of opportunity on Saturday nights from nine to ten in the evening. If we don't have sex then, I'm out of luck!" Catherine said that her body wasn't fully awake in the morning and being sexual wasn't any fun for her. Their arguments about the timing of their intimate moments led them to having more infrequent and less satisfying sex.

Upon hearing about their dissatisfaction with their marriage, I asked, "What are you hoping to change?" and after they both pointed to each other and jokingly said in unison, "Her," "Him," we got down to business. Catherine said, "I want Brent to know that the way I feel isn't a cop-out. I'm really less aroused when I wake up. He has to understand that about me and stop badgering me." Brent said, "She used to be more adventurous and less rigid. Now it's her way or the highway. I'd like the old Catherine back." After reassuring them that their respective sexual preferences were typical of the way many men and women feel—many men's testosterone levels peak in the early morning, whereas for women it's often later in the day—I knew it was time to help them set goals and talk about solutions rather than problems.

I asked Catherine, "When Brent becomes more understanding about your sexual needs, what will he be doing differently?" and she replied, "He'd stop teasing me about that one-hour window of opportunity. It really pisses me off because it's not true. I'm much more open-minded than that. In fact, I'd be willing to have sex in the morning occasionally if he'd stop putting me down for the way I am. It would also be nice if he stayed up later at night a couple of times a week so that we could at least have the chance to be intimate when I want to. Besides, I really like going to bed together sometimes."

Prior to this discussion, all Brent had heard from Catherine was, "I want you to be more understanding," "I want you to know that what I'm saying isn't a cop-out," not exactly clear direction about what to do next. But now Brent heard a more thorough response with infinitely more instructive information: "Quit teasing me, stay up later at night twice a week, and go to bed with me."

I asked Brent a question that was similar to the one I asked Catherine: "When Catherine becomes less rigid, more adventurous, and responsive to your feelings, what will she be doing differently?" and he said, "I sometimes think it's more important for her to get her way than to get along with me. If she were more flexible, she would push herself once in a while to wake up earlier and have a cup of coffee with me in order to wake herself up. It would be nice to spend that time together anyway. She wouldn't have to do this every morning, but one or two times a week would be great." He went on to say, "Lately when we have had sex, there's so much resentment on both our parts. She really hasn't seemed into it for months. She used to be the one to suggest real sensual things like dressing up or trying new positions. She hasn't done that for ages. That's the old Catherine I miss."

Now we were talking. Prior to this conversation, all Catherine heard was, "You're rigid and unadventurous," comments that led not to clarity about solutions but to contempt. With Brent's response, Catherine had some direction. She could wake up and have a cup of coffee with Brent once or twice a week, and she could get out her sexy lingerie and suggest alternative lovemaking positions. That's different, right? As I told you before, when goals are fleshed out solution-oriented style, they contain seeds of solution, and because of that, Brent and Catherine felt more hopeful about turning their situation around.

You are about to read a variety of field-tested marriage solutions. Again, it's important to approach your "home-improvement" project with an experimental eye. Try something. If it works, keep doing it. If not, try something else. Also, I have found it to be a good philosophy to start with the simplest, most direct method first and work your way to more complicated strategies only if necessary.

Straight Talk: Tell It Like It Is

As I mentioned before, one of the most destructive patterns I've seen in marriages is when people become extremely bothered by things their spouses do or say but keep their feelings to themselves. They might try to tell their spouses about their annoyances early on, but if their spouses don't acknowledge their feelings, agree, or change their behavior, they basically give up. Giving up is not to be confused with accepting. Giving up means taking their angry feelings and storing them inside. What happens over time with bottled-up negative feelings? A couple of things.

First, some people harbor negative feelings for weeks, months, even years. Then when the littlest thing happens, it becomes the straw that breaks the camel's back and they explode, big time. Because their reactions seem so extreme, their partners dismiss their complaints, defend themselves, and say, "I bet it's *that* time of the month," or "Oh, did you have a bad day at work today?" Feeling exasperated, they tell themselves never to share their feelings again, and they don't.

This kind of pattern of communication in marriage is the best way to kill feelings of intimacy and closeness. The relationship doesn't feel safe. Marriage feels like two opponents fighting to defend themselves as opposed to two teammates trying to find ways to work together and love each other. People who keep negative feelings inside start building walls around them to protect themselves. Although this wall wards off hurtful feelings, it also blocks feelings of love and intimacy.

Another disadvantage of not speaking your mind is that it allows, even requires, your spouse to call the shots about everything. And eventually, you wake up one day and say to yourself, "My spouse is so controlling. I don't love this person anymore. Everything has to be his [or her] way. I'm not even sure I want to be married. I have lost myself in my marriage. I don't even know who I am anymore."

If feelings such as these have pushed you away from your spouse, making intimacy undesirable, it's essential that you understand your role in creating your monster. If your spouse is bossy and controlling, you've taught him or her that it's okay to be that way by throwing up your hands and letting him or her make all the decisions. You need to learn a better way of standing your ground. You don't have to leave your marriage to take charge of your life; you have to be more forthcoming in your spouse's presence. S/he must know where you stand on important issues. You have to learn how to be more assertive.

This is not to say that you have to confront your spouse every time you're unhappy. In healthy long-term marriages, couples learn how to choose their battles rather than react to every irritating behavior. You first need to ask yourself, "Of all the issues upsetting me, which are the top one or two that must change for me to feel closer to my spouse?" As you identify these issues, make sure you follow the guidelines outlined in the goal-setting section. Think in the action-oriented, positively stated, do-able terms.

Once you have a clear picture of what you want to address, let your spouse know you'd like to have a talk. Before you do, review the guidelines for having constructive conversations in Chapter 8. Once you begin to tell your spouse how you feel about things, you need to notice the difference it makes in your marriage. If being more forthcoming helps, keep doing it. When you do, you'll feel better about you and better about your spouse too.

Wes and Roberta were teetering on the brink of divorce when I met them. They had been separated for eight months. Although they were from the Midwest, they had been living on the East Coast for several years due to Wes's job. Roberta moved back to the Midwest to be closer to family, but Wes had to remain on the East Coast temporarily in order to sell their home. Real estate sales were slow that year, and they weren't able to find a buyer.

During their separation, Wes discovered that he liked his freedom. He worked long hours, had no child care or family responsibilities, and was able to spend as much time at his workout club as he desired. He was beginning to feel torn about his marriage and went to see a therapist. During his therapy, he learned that he had lost himself in his relationship with his wife. She had a strong personality, and he was more laid back. He always seemed to go along with the flow, regardless of whether he agreed with the plan or not. And now his resentment felt all-consuming.

Part of what he recognized in therapy was that he grew up in a household steeped in conflict and anger. He saw how miserable his mother was and decided that when he had a family, he would never allow conflict to ruin his life. As a result, he kept all of his negative feelings inside in his own marriage. He began to resent his wife. When they got together for visits during their eight-month separation, he felt himself shut down completely. He wasn't interested in being together, talking, and least of all, being intimate physically. He had basically given up on his marriage. However, he loved their four-year-old son dearly and as a last-ditch effort decided to try to save their marriage. That's when they came to my office.

When Wes said that he had fallen out of love with Roberta because of her controlling nature, Roberta became tearful and said, "For years, I've been begging you to tell me how you feel. I hate when I ask you if you want to eat Chinese tonight and you say, 'Whatever you want to do.' I hate that you never have an opinion or tell me how you want things done. You always put me in charge of everything. I can handle you disagreeing with me. I *want* you to disagree with me."

Although Wes wasn't certain whether his feelings about Roberta would change, he was willing nonetheless to put effort into changing himself. Their home had sold, and he was ready to move back with his family. I warned Wes that it was going to be challenging to break free from a lifelong habit of avoiding conflict, but that for his sake, Roberta's sake, and the sake of their family, it was extremely important that he do so. He agreed. I sent them home with the homework assignment of paying attention to what was working in their relationship.

Several weeks later, Wes and Roberta returned to my office and appeared considerably happier than when I had last seen them. There were several times when Wes didn't like something Roberta had done or said—she commented on the way he did the laundry and the way he organized his belongings when he returned—and he confronted her on it. Rather than respond with anger or crumble as he feared she might, Roberta took pleasure in Wes's risking sharing his feelings. She thanked him for his honesty. Wes was surprised by Roberta's response. It caught him off-guard. But he found it very reinforcing. In fact, with his new-found permission to stop trying to please Roberta or second-guess her needs and start being himself instead, Wes appeared to feel liberated. You could sense his relief and appreciation for Roberta's support. Clearly, the ice was beginning to melt. They both liked each other more now, a definite first step in healing their marriage.

So, if you're someone who, like Wes, needs to quit pretending and start being real, do it. It may just be the medicine your marriage needs. However, maybe being a straight shooter isn't the key to solving your marital dilemmas. Maybe you've already talked until you're blue in the face. Sometimes in relationships, one person talks and the other tunes out. If you happen to be married to a person who tunes out your words, it may be time to stop talking and start doing something instead.

When it comes to actions that make marriage work, there are two principles that are at the core of every successful relationship: if it works, don't fix it; if it doesn't work, do something different. First, let me tell you what I mean about doing what works.

Do What Works

No matter what kind of relationship problem you might be having with your spouse, there are times when, for a variety of reasons, things go more smoothly. And often a solution to your relationship problems can be found by examining why things go smoothly when they do. It's not just a fluke, even if it feels that way to you. When you experience problem-free or relatively problem-free times, both of you are doing things differently. By doing a little detective work, you can figure this out, and once you do, you can consciously decide to do what works on a more regular basis. Here's an example.

Ida felt herself pulling away from her husband because she was so troubled by his frequent out-of-town business trips. He was gone for long periods of time, and when he was home, they found themselves arguing a great deal. Ida felt that they never had enough time to catch up and feel close to each other. She was not at all interested in being sexual with him under these circumstances.

I asked Ida, "Are there times when your husband travels, but it doesn't seem to take such a toll on your lives?" After considerable thought, she said, "I suppose there are times when he travels but I don't feel quite as disconnected from him as I do now." I wondered what was different about those times, and she said, "I've noticed that if he calls me at least once a day, I feel as though he's thinking of me and that helps. When he comes home, I don't feel so angry." The solution was obvious. Her husband needs to make an effort to call home once a day, perhaps every night to say goodnight. This will go a long way to helping Ida miss him as opposed to resenting his long absences.

Here's another example.

Janice discovered that important conversations with her husband either went extremely well or all hell broke loose. It seemed as if there was nothing in between. But for the life of her, she couldn't unravel the mystery between the two outcomes. However, when we discussed these conversations in detail, it became evident that the more productive conversations had something in common. Rather than bulldoze her husband into talking when she was ready, she asked her husband to pick a time he felt prepared. Every time she did that in advance, things went well. When she bullied him into talking, their conversations spiraled out of control.

You can apply this solution formula to your own situation. Review your relationship goals. Think back to a time when things were a bit more like you're hoping they will be. Ask yourself, What was I doing differently back then? What was s/he doing differently back then? What were we doing differently as a couple? How were we handling things differently? Once you identify the exception, you need to start doing more of what works.

Sometimes people have an idea of what might work, but they stop themselves from doing it because they don't think they should have to be the one to change or because they aren't really feeling motivated to be loving—they're not in the mood. Here's what I have to say about these objections.

If you're a little fuzzy as to why *you* have to be the one to change, it's very simple. You're not the only one who will have to change; your spouse will change too. I am going to teach you strategies that will, in essence, tip over the first domino. When you change how you approach your spouse, s/he will change how s/he responds to you. If you think that one person can't change another, you're dead wrong. You can change your spouse, but you have to begin by changing your own actions first. Don't believe me? I'll prove it to you.

Let's imagine for a moment that you and your spouse are having a wonderful evening together—good conversation, kindness, and laughter. Then for some inexplicable reason, you decide that you want the evening to go downhill, and you want to pick a fight. Could you think of something you could say or do that would effect this change?

Whenever I ask people this question, they start to chuckle and say, "Of course, I know exactly what I would need to do to turn things ugly. I know precisely how to push my partner's buttons." And that's when I say, "Stop. Great. If you know how to push your partner's buttons in a negative way, you can learn how to push his or her buttons in a positive way." I believe that everyone has positive change buttons. You just have to know how to find them and then how to activate them. In the remainder of this section, I'll teach you how to activate your spouse's positive change buttons.

And about not being in the mood to do the things that will bring you closer to your spouse. Although I completely understand how, if you're angry or resentful, you don't really feel like doing relationship-building activities, research shows beyond a shadow of a doubt that the quickest way to change how you feel about something is to take an action. Rather than sit around and wait to feel more conciliatory, taking a small, positive step will help you to feel more conciliatory. For instance, you know that you and your spouse feel closer when you spend more time together. If you're at odds with one another right now, you might not feel like spending time together, so you'll avoid each other. The more you avoid each other, the more distant you feel. However, if you ignore your feelings and push yourself to be together and do things you ordinarily enjoy, you will trigger positive feelings. Time together breeds loving feelings, not just the other way around.

My suggestion to you is that you study what's different about your marriage when things are working. Then, regardless of how you're feeling at the moment, start doing more of what works.

Do Less of What Isn't Working: The Siren Solution

In Chapter 3, you learned about a difference between people: some people need to feel close to their spouses before they're interested in sex, while for others, it's the other way around. They need to feel connected to their spouses sexually before they put effort into being close emotionally.

In the section of this book that addresses your spouse, I will explain the importance of making you feel loved and appreciated if s/he wants you to be more committed to having a better sex life. I will make sure your spouse sees the connection between his or her behavior and how you respond. However, there's another, equally viable way to motivate your spouse to be more loving toward you: you can pay more attention to your sexual relationship. This will make your more highly sexed spouse a much nicer person. Here's an example of how this works.

A while ago I was leading a group for women wanting better relationships. One evening, the women became unusually critical about their husbands, and their discussion bordered on male bashing. "He never talks to me." "He promises to do things with the kids on the weekends, but he turns into a couch potato." "He's always so angry." "I think he's in the throes of a midlife crisis."

I surprised the group by asking a seemingly unrelated question. In the midst of one woman complaining that her husband never completed projects he started around the house, I said, "I'm just curious. I'd like to go around the group and have each of you rate your sex life on a 1-to-10 scale, with 1 being the pits and 10 being great." After a few seconds of blank stares, the scores came rolling in. They were dreadful—Mostly 1s and 2s.

I asked if they would try an experiment. They all agreed. I asked them to go home and for the next two weeks pay more attention to their physical relationships with their husbands. I asked them to be sexier, more affectionate, attentive, responsive, and passionate. I told them to initiate sex more frequently. And then, without offering an explanation, I suggested that they watch closely for any changes in their husbands. I then promptly ended the group. Although they were noticeably surprised by my homework assignment, no one was brave enough to challenge me openly.

Two weeks later, the door to my office opened and in trickled the women, giggling like third graders. Dying of curiosity, I asked, "So how did these two weeks go?" The stories that followed explained their laughter.

One woman said, "I really didn't feel like doing what you suggested, but I did anyway. Even though we had out-of-town guests, I initiated sex several times that week. When they left, I couldn't believe what happened! Of his own volition, he started doing all these projects around the house I had been begging him to do for months. He put up wallpaper, grouted between the tiles in our dining room floor, and made plans for us to go out for dinner, something I always have to initiate! I couldn't believe it!"

Another woman joined in, "My husband hardly ever talks to me about his day. I get so mad at him because he never shares his life with me. Well, I got some new lingerie and was a lot more forward with him sexually. For the next few days, he talked so much, I couldn't get him to stop!" Similar stories followed. It became clear that there was a strong connection between a more active sex life and a husband who had decidedly joined the land of the living.

The women were shocked. They had no idea how powerful the Siren Solution could be. It really isn't rocket science. When you show your love for your spouse by placing more importance on your sexual relationship—even if you're out of practice—you trigger a solution cycle: your spouse becomes happier and more loving in return. And, not surprisingly, you start liking your spouse more and feeling more attracted to him or her, which inspires your spouse to be even nicer back, and so on.

These women learned something else from this experiment. They noticed an additional side benefit to becoming more sexual. Several women said that when their relationships were more intimate emotionally, they felt sexier and more amorous. These women realized that contrary to what they thought, their sexual feelings hadn't disappeared; they were simply camouflaged beneath feelings of frustration and hurt. And now that they were getting along better with their spouses, they rediscovered the siren within.

In the last example, women were the lower-desire spouse. However, if you're a man reading this, you need to know that the Siren Solution, despite its name, is gender blind; it can work just as well for you. If you've been feeling turned off because your wife isn't the nicest person to be around, you might consider giving her a "nice pill" in the form of the Siren Solution. Her changes will amaze you.

SEX SOLUTIONS

The previous techniques focused on things you can do to start feeling closer to your spouse again, a first step in feeling more sexual for so many people. The following techniques are focused more specifically on things you can do to improve your sexual relationship.

The Nike Solution

If you want to boost your desire, consider adopting Nike's wonderful slogan, "Just do it." Are you wondering, "How will having sex with my spouse when I'm not in the mood boost my desire?" Here's how.

You need to remember what I told you before: just because you're not hungering for sex doesn't necessarily mean you have a problem with arousal. Lots of people with low sexual desire actually enjoy sex once they get started. It may take them a while. They may have to clear out the mental clutter and slowly relax, but when they do, they tell me that sex is enjoyable. It's important for you to remember that there is a difference between problems with sexual desire and problems with sexual arousal. You can jump-start your desire by allowing pleasant physical sensations to overpower any reluctant thoughts you might be having about sex.

So, what should you do? Push yourself on a more regular basis to ignore your little inner voice that says, "Oh, no, not now, I'm too tired," or "Again? We just made love two nights ago," or "I've got a million things to do," or, well, you know the rest. Why not just assume that your inner voice is misguiding you? If you enjoy sex once you get started, I really believe that you've unconsciously trained yourself to have "I'm not interested" thoughts every time your spouse touches you. Our minds tend to work in habitual ways. We become conditioned to respond in predictable ways to certain triggers.

If every time your spouse approaches you for sex, you replay the arguments you have had about sex and you start feeling bad, eventually your spouse's touch may trigger in you an instant need to recoil. You don't even need to think about it anymore. It just happens automatically.

But imagine what might happen if you decided to "go for it" more often despite your nagging negative thoughts and allowed yourself to feel the enjoyment. The more you did this, the more you would give yourself opportunities to replace your old thinking habits with a new one. You could link together your spouse's advances with the pleasure you feel once you get going. And when you reinforce *this* link again and again, it becomes stronger and begins to occur naturally. In other words, when your spouse reaches over to touch your hand in an affectionate way, instead of thinking, "There s/he goes again," you might find yourself thinking, "Hm, that feels good." You can retrain yourself to get past your usual objections by focusing on the pleasure you will feel in your spouse's embrace.

There's another reason to "just do it." Some experts in the field of sexuality believe that when it comes to libido, people "use it or lose it." For example, women who remain quite sexually active after childbearing years have higher levels of testosterone. Although one might easily conclude that high levels of testosterone create intensified desire, there is also some speculation that it might work the other way around: that an active sex life triggers testosterone production. The more you do it, the more you want it, the more you do it.

Embers versus Fireworks

In Chapter 2, I told you about a mistake people with low desire often make (Love, 2001). When they think about what it means to desire their spouse, they have unrealistic expectations. They often flash back to the beginning of their relationship when hormones were raging and remember an overwhelming feeling of passion and yearning. Or sometimes they assume that they should feel the same way their more highly sexed partners do—very, very turned on. Neither expectation is particularly valid. Many times, people with lower desire have sexual urges; they're just infinitely more subtle.

For example, you might notice that your husband looks great in his tight jeans and have a fleeting thought about sex. The thought may not linger, but it's there nonetheless. Or you might have read something in a magazine that you found sexy and even noticed some physical sensation inside that feels good. However, it might be subtle and short-lived. If you're trying to improve your desire and sexual relationship, rather than allow these moments to go unnoticed, you should definitely heed them and act on them.

Focus on the Exceptions

I've already explained the importance of focusing on exceptions or the problem-free times in your marriage to find solutions to sticky marital issues. You can use this same method for boosting your desire.

No matter how flat your desire feels at the moment, there are times when you experience a bit more interest. Think about this for a moment. Some people with low desire say that they are somewhat more interested in making love under certain conditions. Perhaps lovemaking is more appealing during certain times of day or month, on the weekends, after a bath or a good talk, on vacation, when the kids are asleep, after you've spent a chunk of time together, when you're feeling good about the way you look, and so on. For example, some people say they feel more amorous late in the day as opposed to early in the morning, or at the middle or end of their menstrual cycles. Some people tell me that they're more interested after a glass of wine or on the weekends. Others tell me that their favorite time is after a relaxed hot bath. Identify what's different about the times you feel more turned on, and take advantage of the moment when you feel more inclined rather than letting it slide. In fact, if it's an option, create the opportunity. In other words, if hot baths turn you on, turn on the hot water more often. Find out what gets your juices flowing and seize the moment.

Know Thyself

If one of the reasons you've been disinterested in sex is that your spouse isn't touching or kissing you in a way that turns you on, you need to be a better coach. Sometimes when I ask people what they would like their spouses to do to light their fire, they're clueless. How can you expect your spouse to know what feels good to you if you don't know yourself?

There's only one way to fix this: become an expert on your own body, which means that you have to start experimenting. Do whatever you need to do to figure out what turns you on. Read romance novels, masturbate, watch sexy movies or videos, use sex toys like vibrators, buy sexy lingerie, use lotions. Everyone is different, so you need to discover the uniqueness of your own sexuality. You need to know if you like hard or soft touches, fast or slow movements or both, depending on the timing. When you're making love, try different positions. See what feels best. Although there are some comprehensive books on this subject (see Recommended Reading), I want you to know two things. First, if you're not feeling turned on, it's *your* responsibility to figure out what might feel more exciting. You're in charge of you. You should read as much as you can about the various ways people make love, and then adopt an experimental attitude. Don't stop trying different things until you hit on something that stirs your interest. And once you figure it out, make sure your spouse knows the magic formula so he can participate. And be flexible. Don't have rigid criteria about the definitions of good sex.

I worked with a man whose wife enjoyed sex and was perfectly capable of having orgasms when he stimulated her clitoris manually but not during intercourse. This troubled him and affected the way he felt about their sexual relationship. This woman loved sex with her husband and wished he wasn't bothered by her inability to "come with him." Once he understood that her not "coming with him" wasn't a sign that he was an inadequate lover—she simply needed more direct stimulation on her clitoris than intercourse allowed—he stopped feeling badly, and their sex life improved.

The other thing you need to keep in mind is that knowing yourself and your sexual preferences is a lifelong endeavor. Just when you find some things that excite you, you might discover that your needs have changed. Life is like that. The only thing you can count on with any assurance is change. Don't get discouraged when your "new solution" stops doing the job. Find some other equally exciting alternative. And as always, keep your spouse informed about your changing desires. Keep the lines of communication open. In Chapter 8, you can learn more about talking about sex with your partner.

Act As If

If you want to feel more sexual, try acting more sexual. Vicki, a forty-two-year-old woman with three children, told me that the key to boosting her interest in sex was for her to do things that she used to do when she felt sexual. She wore sexy lingerie under her clothing and perfume, and she made an effort to dress a bit more seductively. (She loved her tight sweaters.) Vicki realized that she had stopped putting effort into her appearance when she quit feeling sexual. She also discovered that when she forced herself to get out of her dumpy jeans and into her sexy lingerie and clothes, she felt sexier.

Novelty

Even people with low desire become more interested in sex when it is new. Newness is exciting. When you've been married for a while, sex often becomes routine. Routine is boring. If you're bored because you're doing the same old things over and over, you probably won't feel stimulated. You might not reach an orgasm. But you can improve things by changing the way you approach intimacy and lovemaking. You need to become more creative. And if you're not sure how, the recommended books will help you dream up ways to get your creative juices flowing.

If you have depended on your spouse to be the one to breathe new life into your sexual relationship, stop doing that. You are equally responsible for keeping your sexual relationship fresh. Discover new options, and push yourself to have an open mind. You may just surprise yourself.

Ginny was lukewarm about sex but decided it was time to do something about it. She was determined to read several books on the topic. She jokingly referred to her new resolve to restore her passion as Project Desire. Early in her reading (and she had quite a collection of books, I must say), she learned that women have what is known as a G spot, and when it is stimulated, they often have strong orgasms. This was new to Ginny, and she was determined to find her G spot and put it to use. And so she did. Learning new information about how her body worked fascinated her. And although Ginny's husband never joined us for a session, let's just say that I heard through the grapevine that he was a happy man.

The Seesaw Effect

There's something I think you should know. You may not like hearing this, but if none of the desire-building methods have turned you on so far, this one might. Many people tell me that their sex drive returns with a vengeance once their spouses stop being interested in sex. This makes perfect sense when you consider the Seesaw Effect—relationships are such that the more one person does, the less the other will do. The more one person is invested in something, the easier it is for the other to sit back and relax. And this is true about many, many aspects of marriage, including taking out the garbage, making arrangements to get a babysitter, buying birthday cards for family members, or paying bills. We get into roles with our spouses. Then when the person who is doing most of the work stops, it leaves room for the less invested person to step up to the plate and take over. And that's what often happens in regard to sex too.

The problem is that by the time your more highly sexed partner backs off, s/he might be so upset about your marriage that s/he becomes involved in an affair or s/he tells himself that s/he doesn't love you anymore. In other words, by the time you realize how important your spouse is and how much you long for him or her, s/he may be out the door. Take Elyse, for example.

It has been about two years since my husband told me he doesn't love me anymore. Feeling desperate to connect with him, I was positive that he would respond to sex. But when I tried to be sexual, he said, "Don't touch me," and would even pull away. Boy, that was devastating considering I used to say he could be turned on by the color of the wallpaper! That's when I went into sexual overdrive. I was on all the time. A naked toe would set me off. Now I am the insatiable one in the sex department, but he does anything to avoid being touched. I am devastated.

Elyse's renewed sexual passion surprised her. She just didn't think she was a sexual person anymore. But now, Elyse longed to make love. She ached to feel her husband's body close to hers. But for them, her revived passion came too late. Her husband filed for divorce.

Don't let this happen to you. Don't allow the loss of your marriage or your spouse's love or infidelity to be your aphrodisiac. Rediscover your passion for your spouse right now.

Just Say When.

Let's face it, no matter how well these libido-boosting methods work, there will be times when you really just don't feel like having sex. But instead of just saying no or "I'm too tired," which feels like a flat-out rejection to your spouse, offer an alternative. For example, you should say, "I'm really exhausted right now, but if you're willing to wait until I catch a quick nap, I would love to fool around then." Or, "Now isn't great for me, but how about waiting until the kids go to sleep?" You want to do your best so that your spouse doesn't feel rejected. Remember that s/he takes your disinterest personally; it really hurts his or her feelings. As long as you show your spouse that you care about him or her, s/he's more likely to handle your off times with greater understanding.

Give a Gift

One of the biggest mistakes I see less highly sexed spouses make is to assume that if they're not in the mood to be sexual, there's nothing they can or should do to please their spouses. This is craziness. You can show your love for your spouse even if you're not in the mood by doing something that would please him or her sexually. Although I wouldn't recommend an exclusive diet of this, there's nothing wrong with just "taking care of" your spouse.

If you decide to give the gift of being sexual even though your heart isn't completely in it, it's important not to be resentful, or it really isn't a gift at all. This doesn't mean that you have to pretend to be ecstatic or fake breathless orgasms; it just means that you should show some enthusiasm. Whatever you do—whether you offer oral sex, have intercourse, or manipulate your spouse manually—if you do it begrudgingly, it defeats the purpose. Tell your spouse that you'd love to please him or her, and ask what s/he'd like for you to do. Then do it.

This is not to say that you should engage in sexual acts that make you feel uncomfortable or uneasy. You shouldn't be forced or force yourself to do anything that you find unpleasant. But there's nothing wrong with your pushing yourself a little to be a loving sexual partner.

SOME MORE SUGGESTIONS

If you feel you need the help, I have a few suggestions. First, visit my web site, www.divorcebusting.com. You will find an enormous amount of information about making marriages work, and best of all, there is a bulletin board filled with people who are actively working on their relationships. Many of them are dealing with sexual issues just like yours. All of these visitors are focused on finding practical solutions to their marital issues. They are creative and amazingly supportive. And the great news is that the help you receive there is free and accessible 24/7. This comes in handy when you're up in the middle of the night, tossing and turning because you can't get your relationship issues out of your head. You'll find comfort, support, and down-to-earth advice. Plan a visit or two.

If you do want to go to a therapist for help with marital issues but you're cautious about the therapist's experience, skills, or commitment to safeguarding your marriage, you can get more information about finding a qualified therapist by contacting my office at therapistinfo@divorcebusting. com. Don't forget that marriage education is an alternative that many people find more helpful than marriage counseling. You should consider finding a good marriage seminar in your area.

If you would like to see a certified sex therapist—someone who has specific training in dealing with all kinds of sexual issues—contact the American Association of Sex Educators, Counselors and Therapists (AASECT) for a qualified therapist in your area: PO Box 5488, Richmond, VA 23220-0488, www.aasect.org. For a complete list of names to be mailed to you, call the AASECT national office at 804-644-3288.

~III~

The High-Desire Spouse's Guide for Boosting the Marriage Libido

~

CHAPTER FIVE

What About Me?

Although Part Two is aimed at your spouse, I'm assuming that you've read through parts of it and you know that I have encouraged him or her to become a more active and interested sexual partner. I'm also assuming that you have been cheering me on because you've agreed with much of what I've written. As the person with more sexual energy, I know that you have been the forgotten spouse in many ways. Although there is plenty of libido-boosting help available for your spouse, few books have addressed what it's like to be in your shoes. This is especially true if you're a woman, because low desire in men has not been given the attention it truly deserves based on the millions of men struggling with this issue. Be assured that the feelings you've had about your sex-starved marriage are very, very common.

On our twenty-fifth wedding anniversary, I planned a very romantic evening with my husband. He was at work, and I went out and bought new lingerie, some light snacks, the same wine we had the first night we went out, and rented a top-floor hotel room of a five-star hotel near where he worked (since it was midweek and he would have to work the next day). I brought a clean set of work clothes for him for the next day and then left the hotel key, panties sprayed with my perfume, and a note hanging from the visor of his pickup and went back to the hotel to wait. I lit candles all around the room, had music with me, and around 6 P.M. the phone rang. Picture me, giddy with anticipation at how surprised and turned on he will be, and I race to the phone and he says, "What the hell are you doing? I have to work tomorrow!! If you want to get f**ked, can't you wait until the weekend??? I'll see you at home." Never in all my forty-nine years have I felt a blow like I felt that night. I hung up, got drunk, and stayed in the room by myself. He showed up around 4 A.M. and wanted to know why I wasn't home.

I know that your spouse's lack of interest in sex has been challenging for you. You have been questioning your attractiveness and your masculinity or femininity. You've been wondering whether your spouse really loves you. You can't understand how someone could love you and care about your feelings and at the same time reject your advances to make love. It just doesn't make sense to you. Most of all, you've felt isolated in your marriage, which is the worst kind of loneliness a person can feel. You can easily recall the many desperate moments when your spouse has fallen asleep and you lay in bed longing to touch and be touched. You've resented the way your spouse seems to control the relationship, doling out affection on his terms.

As a man, you've been frustrated because your wife thinks you're just a sex maniac or that sex for you is just like scratching an itch. She really hasn't understood how important it is to you to be close to her, to feel her touch, warmth, and love. Although there are undoubtedly those times when sex *is* just a great release, more often than not, it means a lot more than that to you. Having a good sexual relationship with your wife makes you feel whole. The following is from a man whose sexual-intimate relationship with his wife is lacking. As you will see, sex is hardly about just scratching an itch.

Sex in marriage is *very* important to men. After a bad day—maybe losing a job, or a promotion, or anything that really seems to just drag you down—you can always make it better by remembering someone is at home who loves you.

Making love just seems to make everything feel better. It always puts things in perspective. I'd think, "How bad could it be when I'm lying here making love to the woman I love more than anything in the world, and she's making love to me and only me?" That's a huge shot in the arm.

If my wife initiated other forms of affection—a kiss for no reason, lingering a bit when hugging, a look, a smile, or even a knowing smirk—it would take the focus off the lack of making love because those forms of intimacy are even more important than sex sometimes.

It's not the *act* to me. That's the funny thing. I could have had numerous physical affairs, but I never did. More importantly, I never *wanted* to. I'm one of those guys who doesn't fantasize about other women. I love my wife and want her more each day. I want to feel special to the one I love. And when I don't, it affects everything.

And there is another thing your wife probably misunderstands: she probably fails to appreciate how important it is to you to please her sexually and to be a good lover. This essential part of you and your psyche has been denied. You've probably felt a great sense of loss about this, putting even more distance between the two of you.

As a woman, you may totally identify with the man's description above, and you have additional challenges as well. Since the subject of low sexual desire in men is so taboo, your husband has probably shuddered at the thought of talking about it. He probably has recoiled every time you've broached the subject. This is a very sensitive subject for men because it strikes at the very core of their being. Men are taught that real men lust after sex. So to be lustless is to be less than a man. No wonder the word is mum. But many sex therapists believe that low sexual desire in men is vastly underreported. Judging by the couples in my practice and from the mail I receive, I would bet my life on it.

Fortunately, in the last few years, widespread advertising campaigns for drugs like Viagra have allowed men from all walks of life to recognize that sexual problems such as erectile dysfunction are common. Thanks to former senator Robert Dole, *Viagra* has become a household word. However, for a man to feel lustless is a completely different story. It's one thing if your body isn't working the way it should, but quite another if you're just not in the mood. Men without desire often feel flawed, and the shame can present major obstacles for getting help. It's hard to seek professional help for a problem you can't muster up the courage to discuss.

If you're a woman married to a man with low desire, I know you've vacillated between being understanding about his shame and wanting to clobber him over the head for allowing his ego to stand in the way of your having a more loving and vibrant sexual relationship. Does this sound like something you've thought before?

> When women go through pregnancy and menopause and other things that cause hormonal changes, it is considered okay if she lacks the desire. It's even expected. But even in cases of hormonal imbalances in men, low sexual desire isn't okay. The subject is taboo under any circumstance. I don't understand where this attitude in men comes from—why their egos are so dependent on whether they can perform or want to perform. I can't imagine the turmoil inside all the men out there having this problem. They stigmatize themselves for no reason. Bet ya men will be buying *The Sex-Starved Marriage* and taking it home in plain brown wrappers.

Since so few men openly discuss their lack of desire, you might be thinking you're the only woman in the world whose husband isn't interested. That could easily leave you doubting yourself at every turn. But trust me on this one: you're not alone. I have heard from countless women about their husband's lack of desire.

> Nobody knows how much it hurts and does damage to the relationship to be sexually rejected by a man for eighteen years until they have been there. I know my husband wishes I would never bring the topic up again. He would like to live in la-la world where we have a normal marriage even though we never have sex, but not having sex doesn't feel normal to me. I wish I had the guts to leave, but I don't want to break up my family.
>
> I have friends who think I'm lucky that I never have to have sex, but they don't know what it's like to be young and feel sexy and

have the man you're married to take zero interest in making love to you. It sucks.

I feel my husband's lack of interest in sex is tearing my marriage apart. My husband and I are in our mid-twenties and used to have a very busy sex life. Since we married, it has gone downhill rapidly. I am lucky if he will make love to me once every two to three months. I have bought lacy gowns, gone to bed naked, ran around the house in a towel, dressed up, approached him subtly, threw myself at him, and begged, and he almost always rejects me anyway. He doesn't *say* no; he just maneuvers out of the situation or falls asleep. The only time that we do have sex is when we are in bed, with the lights out, and I grope him until he develops an erection. But even then, he won't touch me or do anything to arouse me or kiss me, and a couple of times he has even passed out in the middle.

This is one of the most degrading things that I have ever been through. My self-esteem is high at work and in my outside activities, but the minute that I walk through our front door, I feel ugly and disgusting. I need the intimacy and the closeness and actually even the passion and desire. Without seeing the desire for me in my husband's eyes, I feel worthless.

Regardless of whether you're male or female, the bottom line is that when you believe that you're the only spouse interested in having a good sexual relationship, you feel enormously hurt, angry, and rejected. This is especially true if your sex life was markedly better in the past. Many people tell me that they're furious that their spouses pulled a "bait and switch" gimmick on them. ("Bait and switch" refers to a business practice whereby a business advertises a product at a low price to lure you into the store. Once there, you realize that the advertised product is not available and you're directed to a different product. In short, bait and switch is a ploy to get you into the store.)

A part of me resents my wife for not telling me that she had such a *low* sex drive. She obviously misled me in our courting period to believe that she loved sex as much as I do. I just don't get it. Why do so many women do that? They will transform themselves into this woman that they think you will want, then after getting married, expose themselves for who they really are. Is that being untrue/unfair to themselves too?

If you have been feeling duped, you need to know a few things about your spouse's drop in desire. Without knowing you or your spouse, I can tell you that s/he wasn't trying to fool you into making a commitment by putting on airs about being sexually fired up. The fact is that people with low levels of testosterone tend to feel more energized sexually when relationships are new. Their testosterone levels often spike during these exciting times. Many low-desire spouses look back at the beginning of their relationships as the most sensual and arousing times of their lives. They felt on fire. However, after the newness subsides, so too goes the spike in testosterone along with the desire. The drop in desire is not intentional. It's not malicious. It's not even something low-desire spouses want. It just happens.

And because so few people really understand this, they draw all sorts of erroneous conclusions. More highly sexed folks like you think, "My husband doesn't love me anymore." "My wife isn't attracted to me." "My spouse is obviously in love [or having sex] with someone else." At the same time, your spouse has equally erroneous thoughts: "Maybe I've fallen out of love." "There must be something wrong with our marriage." "Why can't my spouse turn me on anymore?"

If you read Chapter 2—and it's a must—you should know there are lots of reasons a person can lose desire, and some of them have absolutely nothing to do with you. It may be all about fluctuating hormones or challenging personal issues. Yet I bet you have spent countless hours trying to figure out what you've done wrong or why you're not desirable. I hurt so much for couples in my practice when I hear them groping for explanations that are self-defeating and damaging to their relationships.

Suffice it to say, you are different from your spouse. You're even wired differently. Your brains work differently. Although you might think about sex on and off many, many times throughout the day, your spouse may think of it only when the calendar tells him or her, "It's *that* time," once again. While you may be easily turned on by countless triggers—the scent of perfume, a sensual glance, a low-cut or tight-fighting shirt—your spouse may require a slew of conditions to get revved up: a quiet home, the bills paid, kids asleep, chores done, the lawn mowed, and a good talk that day. What comes easily to you may take work and effort for your partner. Even if s/he has an orgasm each time you make love, it may take your spouse so much energy to get there, it just doesn't seem quite worth the effort.

As the more highly sexed spouse, I know it must be hard for you to fathom how your spouse could feel that way or why a person would not want to do something that in your eyes is so exciting, pleasurable, and satisfying. I know you've been having a hard time making sense of this whole dilemma; that there have been times when you're convinced your spouse is just punishing you or trying to control the relationship. But you need to stop thinking this way. If you're going to make any headway in regard to your desire gap, you are going to have to quit making assumptions and start doing a better job of understanding what is really going on inside your spouse's heart and mind. Why?

Earlier in this book, I spent a great deal of time "talking" to your spouse, explaining the importance of a robust sexual relationship and why you—the more highly sexed spouse—are feeling the way you do about sex. I recognize that if your relationship is to improve, your spouse has to develop a deeper understanding about the role sexuality plays in marriage.

But empathy and understanding must be a two-way street. You need to appreciate better what it's like to be inside your spouse's mind and body too. You need to have more compassion for what it might feel like to have a questionable sex drive in a sex-crazed world. You also need to recognize that when you ask your spouse, "What's wrong?" "Why aren't you interested in sex anymore?" and s/he doesn't answer to your satisfaction, your spouse isn't trying to be evasive. S/he may be as clueless as to the origin of low sexual desire as you are. You need to stop getting angry when you hit a dead end and approach this matter more patiently, lovingly, and collaboratively.

In Chapter 7, I offer you many ideas about new ways to approach your spouse to motivate him or her to become a more active sexual partner. But before you fast-forward to that chapter, I want you to have a better understanding of the role you play when it comes to improving your sexual relationship. If you've been thinking, "There's nothing I can do because the ball is in his or her ballpark," you're wrong. Even if your spouse's low desire is due to off-the-charts low testosterone or a rotten childhood—conditions that have absolutely nothing to do with you—how you approach this very sensitive subject can make all the difference in the world.

Review Chapter 2, where I describe the reasons people experience low sexual desire. The list of potential causes of low desire is so long it's a wonder that anyone is in the mood ever!

Try to envision what it would be like to rarely or almost never desire another person sexually or think sexual thoughts. And while you're at it, picture yourself masturbating and your mental movie goes blank, or your touches don't feel sensual or exciting. Or imagine that your feelings of excitement are so fleeting that it's hard not to feel frustrated. What would it be like for you knowing that millions of people are easily turned on but you feel deader than a doorknob? How would you feel about your body failing you in this way?

And speaking of bodies, what if you didn't like yours? What if you felt shame or embarrassment at the thought of your spouse seeing you naked in the light of day? How easy would it be for you to relax and feel pleasure? Imagine, too, that you feel pain during intercourse, that orgasms are few and far between, your erections don't happen or don't last very long: How eager would you be to initiate sexual encounters? Or what if you were in constant physical pain or felt ill much of the time? How enticing would sex be then? Would you be lusting after your partner or focusing on ways to alleviate your discomfort?

And then there are depression, stress, and sheer exhaustion. What if you felt so overwhelmed, uptight, and on edge that switching gears and letting go was something you just couldn't fathom doing? Would you be fantasizing about frisky evening romps in bed—or longing for the comfort of sleeping alone?

And taking this a bit further, what if your spouse, the person you love the most, your life partner, had absolutely no understanding or appreciation for what you're going through? What if s/he kept telling you about his or her unhappiness in the marriage, that you're a sexual disappointment—an ice queen or a wimp. How do you think you would feel about it?

Look, I know you're unhappy about the differences in your sexual appetites, but you need to know that you're not alone; your spouse isn't having a picnic either. Given the choice, your spouse wouldn't opt for this chasm between you; you'd be more on the same wavelength. Even if your spouse appears cold-hearted or uncaring about your feelings, it's just a defense. Inside, s/he's hurting just as you are. It's no fun knowing you've fallen short in the eyes of a person you love.

There's another reason you need to look inside yourself. Your spouse's lack of desire might be due to marital stress or discord. If so, your willingness to acknowledge your contribution to the problems and change yourself becomes paramount. A more loving marriage may be the only aphrodisiac your marriage really needs. So don't be too quick to point fingers or sit back and put your feet up. You've got work to do. Let me give you an example.

The following story is about a woman who transformed from a low-desire spouse into an extremely enthusiastic lover when she was treated with more love and affection. Unfortunately, she learned what it takes to build desire the hard way: she ended her marriage. If she had made the connection between a more loving marriage and a fiery sexual appetite sooner, she and her ex-husband might still be married. Nonetheless, this woman's example demonstrates that you aren't either a "high-desire" or "low-desire" person, but rather, that desire can fluctuate greatly depending on the quality of your marriage.

My ex-husband and I were married in college, had two children, and successful careers. We lasted twenty-two years. At the beginning of our marriage, sex was frequent, and there were no problems. Then came the children, the pressures of our careers, and then the affairs. He always had a temper, and as the years went by, it got worse. Although he was never physically abusive, his words often were. I could never do anything right or to his satisfaction.

It was like leading a double life for me. Professionally, I excelled, was confident and competent. At home, it seemed I was a total failure in my husband's eyes. As his job became more demanding and stressful, he became more demanding of me. My interest in sex waned. It would occur once a week, basically because I didn't want to battle with him. For me, it was strictly a physical act, and I was detached from it. I figured he was lucky to be getting something, so I wasn't particularly creative or giving sexually. My ex-husband accused me of being frigid. In spite of everything, I loved my husband, and I was baffled as to why I had so little desire to be intimate with him.

Now, years later, I'm no longer baffled. I learned that lovemaking starts outside the bedroom. To have a good sex life, your marriage has got to be good as well. First and foremost, there was the problem of trust. I had built this wall of safety around me so that he wouldn't hurt me, and I could never fully give myself to him. He didn't know my innermost feelings or me. Frankly, he wasn't interested because he was too wrapped up in himself. The intimate connection was missing.

The other thing that was a major factor was his attitude toward me outside the bedroom. He was nasty up to an hour or so before bedtime; then he'd become sweet. But by then, I wanted nothing to do with him. I would stall doing all kinds of things around the house hoping he'd fall asleep before I got there. I grew depressed and felt trapped. My marriage was a living hell, and we divorced.

I have since met and married a wonderful man. This man is the most honest and truthful person I have ever met. I have learned to trust. He is loving, caring, and always considerate. This man makes love to me all day long *outside* of the bedroom. I have been able to give myself totally to him. There is not a thing he doesn't know about me or me him.

As a result, I have found a sexual side to me that I did not know existed. With him, I *want* to be experimental. I look forward to making love and find it very satisfying. We make love five to six times a week. Although I didn't like oral sex before, now it actually turns me on and gets me excited. It has become a big part of our lovemaking. Anal sex still doesn't do much for me, but I don't mind it, and because I know he likes it, I want to give that to him. *I'm* the one who suggests it. We have a wonderful sex life. I never knew it could be like this. I feel sexier than ever.

I share this story with you to illustrate a few extremely important points. As a more highly sexed spouse, you might have an easier time separating feelings of emotional closeness from sexual pleasure. Even if things aren't perfect between you and your spouse, you might still be happy to jump in bed. In fact, you might feel fairly certain that an hour in bed is the fastest way to fix whatever might be ailing your marriage.

But your spouse has got things turned upside down. Your relationship must be nurturing, comforting, and enjoyable *before* sex is a consideration. Your spouse might need to be intimate emotionally—spend time together, talk about personal matters, make eye contact, share the ins and outs and ups and downs of your days, and so on—in order to feel turned on. In short, sharing yourselves on a personal level allows your spouse to feel a bond that triggers sexual desire.

But here's the catch. (If you didn't read about this dilemma in Chapter 3, you will now.) Despite the fact that your spouse might need to feel closer to you in order to desire you sexually, you may not feel like doing what it takes to make that happen. You probably have been feeling so frustrated, hurt, and angry that you don't really feel up to talking, relaxing together, or going on dates. The only talk *you* feel like having is about your paltry sex life.

You don't need a degree in psychology to see why you and your spouse have been going in circles. Your spouse is waiting for you to show more interest in him or her, and you're waiting to be touched. And the problem is that even if you've had fleeting thoughts about stretching yourself and meeting halfway, you've stopped dead in your tracks because you've told yourselves, "I'm just not in the mood." Can you say, "standoff"?

You might be completely justified in feeling angry, resentful, and hurt, but if you continue to allow those feelings to give rise to your actions, you're in big trouble. I can't tell you how many times people with low desire have told me, "When my wife nags or criticizes, I can't stand being around her, let alone make love to her," or "My husband is so angry, I always feel as if I'm walking on eggshells. I never feel safe enough to let my guard down and relax." If you want your spouse to come closer, *you* are going to have to change.

I really want you to take stock of your behavior. Have you been highly critical or bossy? Out of anger, have you berated your spouse or been mean-spirited? Have your feelings of resentment about your sex life prompted you to shut down emotionally and pull away from your spouse? Do you intentionally make plans that don't include your husband or wife? Do you feel yourself building a wall around you to protect yourself from feelings of rejection? Are you feeling tempted to stray beyond your marriage to find companionship and sexual excitement?

If you've answered yes to any of these questions, you have to get a grip on yourself and decide whether *you're* willing to make the kinds of necessary changes to increase the odds that your spouse will share your enthusiasm for creating a better, more dynamic love life. If you've been angry and resentful and you're having a difficult time envisioning yourself letting go, know that holding grudges is a sure-fire way to keep things status quo. Pointing fingers and keeping score hasn't gotten you very far. Just keep in mind that you can't change the past, no matter how hard you try, but you can create your future. And you have to start by changing your own actions. The next chapter will show you how.

CHAPTER SIX

The Harder I Try, the Worse Things Get

Have you ever thought to yourself, "The more I try to improve our sex life, the worse it gets?" or "The more I want sex, the less s/he does?" If so, you're feeling frustrated, and so you will really want to read this chapter carefully because I am going to explain how this seesaw phenomenon happens.

When we encounter a problem in life, we do something to eliminate it. If things improve, life goes on. If things don't improve as a result of our efforts, instead of saying to ourselves, "That didn't work. It must be time to do something completely different," we usually say to ourselves, "What I'm doing isn't helping. I guess I haven't tried hard enough." And then we make the mistake of continuing to do what hasn't been working, only now we redouble our efforts and do it more emphatically, with more passion. And guess what happens when we do more of what hasn't been working? If you thought, "It still doesn't work," you'd be right. But there's one more thing you should consider. When you do more of the same, not only will you fail to improve things, you will actually make your situation worse. Let me give you an example.

I worked with a couple who was having major marital problems. The wife was depressed because her husband had withdrawn from her emotionally. In order to lift her spirits, she would often go shopping. Unfortunately, she was married to the world's most frugal man who, when she shopped, would go into a major funk and withdraw even more. The more she shopped, the more he pulled away from her. The more he pulled away from her, the more she shopped.

In reading this story, it appears obvious that this woman should have noticed that her husband was pulling away even more each time she went to the mall. Conversely, her husband should have noticed that his isolationist behavior was prompting his wife to make extravagant use of the credit card. They both should have instructed themselves to do something to break free from the vicious circle. But that's not what happened. Instead, she continued to "shop until he dropped," and vice versa. Now, let's apply this dynamic to the problem of desire discrepancy.

MORE OF THE SAME BEHAVIOR #1— CAT AND MOUSE GAME

Perhaps when you pursue your spouse to be sexual, your spouse turns you down repeatedly. These rejections might prompt in you a single-mindedness about getting your spouse to be a willing partner. The more your spouse doesn't seem interested in sex or desirous of you, the more you think about sex. (It's like becoming obsessed with food the minute you decide to go on a diet.)

Because you grow "obsessed" with being connected sexually, you find it impossible to have day-to-day interactions without turning them into opportunities to be sexual; you turn a run-of-the-mill goodbye kiss in the morning into a tongue-thrusting sexual kiss. When you hug, you find yourself rubbing your spouse's genitals. You pass in the hallway, and you brush your hand against your spouse's thigh. You talk on the phone and interject sexual innuendoes. Now, pressured by your frequent sexual overtures, your spouse feels annoyed rather than turned on. Instead of noticing this undesirable effect, you forge ahead. You keep on keepin' on. And the more you pursue, the more your spouse withdraws.

One might think that this would prompt you to reevaluate your game plan and consider a new approach. But that's not what happens. Instead, you decide to discuss your unhappiness with your spouse. In other words, you pursue even more. Feeling even more cornered and overwhelmed, your spouse may shut the door on any closeness, physical or otherwise. Even a blind man can see the gridlock of this highly ineffective more-of-the-same behavior.

Often, the very thing you do to *solve* a problem—the strategy you use or the coping mechanism that comes naturally to you—is what's actually prompting your partner to dig in his or her heels. Now, your spouse's twinges of sexual desire might be extinguished by the push-pull dynamic in your relationship. Although the differences in your sexual desire might have been minor at one point, this dynamic can make you and your spouse miles apart over time. I've seen this happen time and time again in my practice.

If doing more of the same has such a negative impact, you might be wondering why you and everybody else you know keeps doing the same old thing. That's a good question. The problem is, as with the shopping woman and her depressed husband, that people rarely recognize how their behavior actually affects their partners. This kind of myopia is common. You are blinded to the ways in which your actions are triggering your partner to do more of what you don't like. And because you fail to see the connection between your actions and an escalation on the part of your spouse, you just assume your spouse is getting more and more stubborn and less and less caring about your feelings. In other words, the deterioration of your relationship appears to be entirely your spouse's fault, and you're just the innocent bystander. Therefore, you don't question your actions or the assumptions you're making about your situation.

Another reason people persist in doing more of the same despite lousy results is that the approach they're taking to solve problems is usually the most logical thing to do. Their actions make perfect sense given the dilemma at hand, so, it makes questioning the validity of their strategies very unlikely. This is unfortunate because as you're about to discover, logic doesn't always work. Even if you think your approach is right and that it should be effective, it doesn't mean it's going to yield the results you want. Remember this, because it's probably one of the most important lessons you'll learn here. You can be "right" and utterly miserable.

One of the reasons more of the same doesn't work is that it causes you and your spouse to go into automatic pilot: you know exactly what you're going to say and do, and you know precisely what your spouse is going to say and do in return. Your spouse has you figured out too. Because you've memorized your interactions, you don't have to pay attention. You just press the Play button and let 'er roll. You're not listening to your spouse, and your spouse isn't listening to you. You're just having knee-jerk reactions, and when you're having a relationship problem, responding without thinking doesn't work very well. That's why nothing ever changes.

Have you been doing more of the same? Have your efforts to spice up your sex life resulted in a blander, less loving, and even less frequent sexual relationship? If so, I know what you've been thinking. You've been telling yourself that your spouse is all to blame, that whatever is causing your spouse to reject your advances has taken an even stronger hold on him or her. If your theory is that low testosterone is to blame, you're assuming testosterone levels have dropped even further. If you think depression is the culprit, you believe the depression has worsened. And truth be told, you may be entirely right. But there may be another piece of the puzzle that you're overlooking and that's you. Despite your best intentions, the very things you're doing to bring your spouse closer may be pushing him or her away. And because you're right in the middle of things, it's often very hard to see the impact of your own behavior. So, I'm going to help you try to look at yourself a bit more objectively.

When couples in my practice have a desire gap, there are a number of places I see them getting stuck doing more of the same. The first, and most obvious, is the one I described above: when one partner pursues sex/intimacy/affection, and the other withdraws. Although this is by far the most common pattern, there are others that might be familiar to you too. As you read through them, think about your interactions with your spouse. If the scenarios sound familiar, it's time for you to rethink your approach to things.

MORE OF THE SAME BEHAVIOR #2— "WHAT'S WRONG?"

Have you asked your spouse many probing questions—"Is something wrong?" "Aren't you attracted to me anymore?" "We used to make love every night. Why aren't we doing this anymore?"—hoping to shed light on his or her feelings about your sexual relationship? As you think about it, what has your spouse's response been to your questions? Although I know that you're just trying to understand things better, does your spouse accuse you of "interrogating" him or her and, as a result, pull away from you? If so, you need to stop asking so many questions.

MORE OF THE SAME BEHAVIOR #3— THE GREAT DIAGNOSIS DEBATE

It's Thursday night. You're home watching the news on television. By chance, you catch a sex therapist talking about the causes of low sexual desire. You think, "This is great. We're going to get free advice from an expert," so you're all ears. Then the expert says what you've thought all along: "Sexual desire and depression don't mix very well." For months, you've been thinking that your spouse is depressed, so hearing your theory validated makes you feel giddy with hopefulness. "At last," you tell yourself. "I knew I was right about this. I just knew my spouse is depressed. No wonder s/he's been asexual. Now that we know what the problem is, s/he can get help for depression, and we can get our lives back on track." And you rush into the kitchen to share the news.

But lo and behold, your spouse doesn't share your enthusiasm for the discovery because s/he doesn't think s/he is depressed. Your spouse thinks his or her sexual desire has vanished because s/he's overworked, underappreciated, and resentful. And no matter how much you disagree or cite the expert you just heard on television, it doesn't make one bit of difference. Your spouse sees things differently. If you continue to try to convince him or her about the reasons sex has become a problem in your lives, you'll make improvements in your sex relationship an even more unlikely prospect.

When it comes to the diagnosis debate, the following are some of the typical topics about which couples argue. Read through them to see if any of them sound familiar. If so, you simply have to quit debating. It's making things worse. Think about it as the who, what, why, and when of diagnosis debates.

Who

Couples often argue about who is to blame for the problems in the marriage. When it comes to a desire gap, the more highly sexed spouse—you—usually thinks that the unhappiness in the marriage is your partner's fault. You believe that your spouse has low sexual desire and that s/he must change. Your spouse might not agree that s/he has low desire. S/he might think that *you* are oversexed and that sex is just too important to you. Your spouse might believe that if you would just back off or stop making such a big deal out of sex, everything would be okay.

When couples argue about who's to blame, both partners expect the other spouse to change first. They reason, "If I'm right, why should I be the one to change?" Christine and Daniel were living examples of this kind of resistance.

Christine and Daniel had major disagreements about their sexual relationship. Daniel wanted more, and Christine wanted less. They were having sex once or twice a month. Daniel would have preferred to be intimate every day. For Christine, twice a month was a stretch. Daniel would complain often, and Christine was very unhappy as well. Both blamed the other for their unhappiness.

Daniel was intent on convincing Christine that their marital problems were due to her lack of sexual desire. He wanted to prove to her that her desire was abnormal so that she would do something about it. When he failed to convince Christine that she had a problem, he surveyed his friends and presented Christine with the results, which favored his position. Christine was enormously unimpressed. "I could care less what your friends are doing with their wives," she would say. "I spoke to my friends, and they're all having sex about as often as we are."

Still certain that he was right about their "infrequent" sex, he did a search on the Internet to gather more concrete information to sway Christine. He discovered a number of articles reporting that the average number of times most Americans have sex is once or twice a week. Relieved to discover the "hard data" he needed to prove his point, he sat Christine down and read the results out loud. Unmoved by his evidence, Christine replied, "I don't really give a damn what your articles say. There is nothing wrong with me. You're the one with the problem."

Daniel was frustrated. He knew he was "right," but it didn't make a bit of difference to Christine. He couldn't believe how incredibly stubborn she was being, refusing to look at herself and her behavior. "Deep inside," he told himself, "she must know she's wrong." And he continued to explore other resources to prove to it to her. What do *you* think the chances are of his succeeding?

What

Even if you both agree that sex is a problem or that your spouse's libido is lacking, you both undoubtedly have elaborate theories as to what might be causing this problem. Often these theories are highly incompatible. You might think it's menopause or problematic hormones, while your wife believes it to be your critical nature. You might think it's your husband's midlife crisis, but he thinks it's due to the fact you've been nagging or that you've allowed yourself to get out of shape. You may believe that side effects from medications have robbed your spouse's desire and you've been urging him or her to see a doctor, but your spouse may think that his or her drop in desire is due to the normal aging process. Trying to force your spouse to see the light won't do a bit of good.

Why

Even if you agree about the cause of low sexual desire, you might disagree about the reasons the causes came into existence. For example, let's say you both believe that depression is at the root of a low desire. You might think that your spouse is depressed because of biological factors (there is a history of family depression), whereas your spouse might believe that the depression is caused by dissatisfaction with work. Although you might feel certain medication is mandatory, your spouse might not be willing to investigate medical solutions. Your spouse might think a job change would do him or her a world of good.

Any change is a good change. Don't argue about the direction of the change. Just be grateful something new is being tried. Don't debate about it.

When

There are two common arguments in this category. The first involves the issue of how frequently couples actually have sex. When couples with a desire gap discuss sexual frequency, it's hard to believe that they are even in the same relationship. Something as quantifiable as the number of times each week they make love becomes a major disagreement. One spouse thinks they make love once every seven to ten days, while the other thinks it's more like once a month. How is this possible?

If you frequently feel rejected, it might leave you feeling that "you never have sex," whereas your spouse's diminished sexual needs coupled with an omnipresent awareness about the troublesome sexual issues between you might leave him or her feeling as if you're having sex all the time. Obviously, your respective lenses distort reality. You both end up feeling you're right.

The second "when" argument has to do with the timing of your lovemaking. Maybe as far as you're concerned, the best kind of sex is spontaneous—when the passion moves you. But for your partner with lower desire, it might be different. S/he might have a list of conditions that have to be in place if sex is going to occur. Couples often argue about the validity and fairness of these preconditions or whether they're just attempts to avoid being sexual.

MORE OF THE SAME BEHAVIOR #4— THE MOTIVATING MISTAKE

Let's say you and your spouse agree there's a problem, and you even agree about the cause of the problem. This doesn't guarantee that your spouse will be motivated to do anything about it. How you go about trying to inspire your spouse might help or hurt your chances for change. If constant reminders to schedule a doctor's appointment, go to the gym, talk to a sex therapist, take medication, and so on have fallen on deaf ears, you might be alienating your spouse more than you are helping him or her. The only time you should offer frequent reminders is when they work. If your spouse appreciates your thoughtfulness, keep reminding. Otherwise, your "helpfulness" may be backfiring. Watch for this.

QUESTIONS TO ASK

If, after reading these common more of the same dilemmas, you're still uncertain where you're getting stuck, ask yourself the following questions:

- *What have I been doing, saying, or thinking on a regular basis about the sexual problems between my spouse and me?*

When you answer this question, make sure that your responses are in action-oriented terms. For instance, don't say, "I've been pushy"; say, "I've been asking many questions about her feelings, and she is starting to get angry at me." Don't say, "I have been frustrated with him"; say, "I have been telling him that I don't want to live like this anymore. I have been getting him names of therapists and urging him to go."

- *Is what I'm doing working or pushing my spouse further away?*

If the answer to this question is "pushing my spouse further away," you've hit the nail on the head. This is the more of the same behavior you need to stop doing.

If you haven't quite figured out your more of the same behavior, it may be because you're too close to it to recognize it. If so, ask yourself this:

- *What would my spouse say that I've been doing or saying lately in regard to our sexual differences that is absolutely driving him or her nuts?*

Be honest. Remember that you don't have to agree with your spouse; you just have to identify what you're doing that is pushing your spouse's buttons.

*   *   *

Now comes the hard part. You have to agree that even if you're right, even if you have your marriage's best interest at heart, you are going to quit doing more of the same. Now that you've identified what you're doing that isn't working, you can no longer pretend that you're trying to make things better when you do it. If you aren't helping the situation with the way you're handling it, you're hurting it. Don't forget that. You have got to try a new way to get through to your spouse and make your sexual relationship better. The next chapter will show you how.

CHAPTER SEVEN

Melting the Ice

Now that you have a more thorough understanding about what's going on with your spouse and you have identified the things you're doing that have kept you at a stalemate, it's time to find solutions. This chapter will help you figure out what you can do differently to motivate, encourage, and support your spouse's efforts to make having a good sexual relationship a bigger priority.

If you are a goal-oriented person, this chapter will provide welcome relief since it will offer lots of suggestions. And speaking of being goal oriented, although I tackled the topic of solution-oriented goal setting in Chapter 4, you may not have read it because that chapter was geared toward your spouse. Therefore, I will tell you a little bit about solution-oriented goal setting right now. You and your spouse have been going in circles for so long that you need to know what to look for when you start breaking out of the circle.

I can just hear you saying, "But, Michele, I know what my goal is: I want a better sex life." To begin with, that's not a clear or concise enough goal. In fact, for now, it's even a little bit too ambitious. Why? I'm going to make a guess about you and your spouse. You've probably tried to get him or her to understand the importance of a good sexual relationship for some time now. For a variety of reasons, your spouse probably hasn't been all that receptive. In short, you've been stuck at square one, and you don't go from square one to having a satisfying sex life overnight. There are many steps in between. I'm going to help you figure out the baby steps so you can tell when you're pointed in the right direction. So start by getting out a pen and piece of paper and jot down your goals. Ask yourself, What do I want to change or improve about my sexual relationship? Now, take a look at your response. Make sure it takes the following three criteria into account:

1. State your response positively.

If you're like most other people, when I ask what you're hoping to change about your sexual relationship, you've probably responded with a complaint rather than describe what you'd like to see happen. For example, you might have said, "My wife never seems interested anymore," or "We have no sexual relationship," or "I wish he weren't so tired all the time." If you complained, I understand why, but you're going to have to turn your complaint into a request for change. Here's how.

Let's say your response is, "My wife never seems to be interested anymore." Ask yourself, "When my wife starts being interested, what will she be doing that she isn't doing now?" One possible response might be, "My wife will be receptive when I kiss her in the evening," or "She will give me a compliment about my appearance once in a while, like she used to do." If your response was something like, "I wish he weren't so tired all the time," ask yourself, "When he starts having more energy, what specifically will he be doing that he hasn't been doing recently?" You might respond, "He will snuggle with me on the couch."

2. State your response in action-oriented terms.

Many people's goals are too vague. Vague goals make success less likely. Examples of vague goals might be, "I would like a more active sex life," or "I want my partner to be more passionate when we make love," or "I want to make love, not have sex." Although *you* may know what you mean when you say things like this, your spouse might not. If you want to give your spouse a running chance to meet your needs, you have to be extremely clear about what you want him or her to do. Clear goals are action oriented; they include descriptions of the actions you and/or your spouse will take to improve things.

If your stated goals are, "I would like a more active sex life," or "I want my partner to be more passionate when we make love," or "I want to make love, not have sex," you have to ask yourself, "When this happens, what will we be *doing* differently?" Make sure your responses are behaviors you can see or hear on videotape. For instance, translate, "I would like a more active sex life," into, "Currently, we have sex once every two weeks. I would like to have sex two or three times a week." Translate, "I want my partner to be more passionate when we make love," into "I want to make love looking into each other's eyes. I want you to stroke my hair and let me know you're excited by being more vocal." Translate, "I want to make love, not have sex," into, "I would like more foreplay. I love when you rub my back before we have intercourse. Please say intimate things to me like, 'I love you. You're very important to me.'"

3. State your response in small, do-able steps.

Your goals should be stated in terms of actions you can accomplish within a short period of time, such as a week or two. If your sexual relationship is nonexistent, rather than aim at having sex once or twice a week, which may be your ultimate goal, think about the baby steps in between. Ask yourself, "What will be the *very first* signs that things are moving in the right direction?" In this case, they might be, "My husband will agree to read the article I gave him on the side effects of medications on sexual desire," or "I will be able to discuss my concern about our marriage without my wife's becoming defensive. She will tell me that she understands how I feel," or "My husband will be willing to schedule an appointment with his doctor for a complete check-up." Remember, one step at a time. You have to be realistic. Now, go back to your goals and make sure that they fit the three solution-oriented criteria. If not, adjust them.

Another thing you need to know before you proceed to solutions is that people go through a six-stage process when they make big life changes (Prochaska, Norcross, and DiClemente, 1994). Although how long a person or couple spends in each stage varies, and some people skip stages entirely, this guide will help you know what to expect in the weeks and months ahead.

1. Acknowledge there's a problem.

Your spouse has to acknowledge that your desire gap has created real problems in your marriage. It's not necessary for your spouse to believe that s/he is the problem, just that the marriage is rocky because of the differences in your levels of sexual desire. Acknowledging the problem can be a difficult step, especially if you and your spouse have been arguing a lot about this subject. Admitting there's a problem might feel like giving in. No one likes to lose face, as petty as that might seem. And although this is not a matter of right and wrong, it can still feel that way.

Another reason your spouse might be slow to acknowledge this problem is that s/he might have to confront painful or uncomfortable issues about him/herself or about your relationship. For instance, if your spouse's lack of interest in sex has to do with past traumatic experiences, you can understand that the prospect of opening up that can of worms is not too appealing. Similarly, if what's gotten in the way of your spouse's libido is a serious yet unaddressed marital issue, you can imagine how scary it might be to begin tackling the problem. For people who have a hard time facing challenging personal or interpersonal issues, avoidance is the method of choice.

And finally, if you're a woman whose husband has little desire, I can't emphasize enough how difficult it is for men to face this issue inside themselves, let alone with you or, worse yet, publicly. The shame they may feel can be overwhelming. In the end, your husband will need to step up to the plate and deal with it, but it's hard, and that may be the reason he's procrastinated. Hopefully, with your help, he'll find a good reason to acknowledge what's really going on.

2. Be willing to do something about it.

Knowing there's a problem is one thing. Doing something about it is another. Your spouse must get to the point where s/he believes that it's necessary to begin addressing this problem in some way.

3. Gather information.

Many people feel the need to research the subject of low desire or desire discrepancy before doing something about it. They will read books, articles, search the Internet, talk to others, and so on. Although this information-gathering stage might not produce a direct result on your sex life just yet, know that it is very important to some people and that it is, in itself, action—plus, it leads to the next, even more action-oriented stages.

4. Decide on a path.

For some, "diagnosing the problem" is a prerequisite for deciding how to proceed. Because low desire can stem from biological, emotional, and relational factors, there are many different places to begin. Your spouse has to decide what makes most sense to him or her. As long as your spouse does *something,* you will be a lot further along than you have been. You may not agree with your spouse's diagnosis of the problem or choice of treatment. If I were you, I'd keep my opinions to myself. Rather than debate the "right" way to handle things, be thankful that your spouse is becoming more proactive, and support those efforts to change, even if it means doing something with which you don't totally agree. It is important to keep in mind that many roads lead to Rome. Furthermore, if you don't put up resistance, if your spouse's plan fails, s/he will see you as an ally rather than a foe and might ask for help on the next plan of action. Be cooperative.

Beyond being cooperative, you should also be appreciative of your spouse's efforts to change. And I don't just mean inside your heart. You should voice your appreciation loudly and clearly, even if you think you shouldn't have to do that. The best way to shape someone's behavior is to reinforce good behavior positively when you see it happening. You want to encourage your spouse's doing what it takes to bring back the passion. *Anything* s/he does toward this end should prompt you to bring on the fanfare. Tell your spouse, "I can't tell you how much I appreciate your_____[going to the doctor, reading this book, changing your medication]." And thank your spouse even if you don't think you should have to.

5. Experiment.

This is the stage when you and your spouse take action—the stage for which you've been waiting. Although you might feel relief that your spouse is finally "doing something," I can't stress enough the importance of your recognizing that stages 1 through 4 represent your spouse's doing something too. You must crawl before you walk. Consider the early stages crawling.

You must be patient. Even if you think you've already waited forever, if you truly want to give your new desire-boosting program a chance, remind yourself to take things slowly. It's the only way to speed up the process.

6. Maintain the changes.

Once you and your spouse have experienced positive changes in your sexual relationship and you're feeling closer to each other, you will have to keep doing whatever you've been doing that has worked. You will need to make being more sexual a way of life. And no matter how much you believe that the success of this endeavor rests on your spouse's shoulders, it doesn't. A good sexual relationship is a two-person job. If your spouse has put effort into being more sexual, you've been doing something to promote and inspire him or her. You've got to keep doing it.

FIRST THINGS FIRST

Now that you have an overview of how change will occur, it's time for you to begin approaching the issues in your sexual relationship in a new way. The desire-boosting methods included here have been "field-tested" by couples in my clinical practice; they work. Since many sexual stalemates are due to rocky relationships, some of the methods you'll read about here are designed to help the two of you get along better in general. The idea is that once your spouse feels closer to you emotionally, s/he will want to be closer physically. Other sexual stalemates have more to do with the specific ways two people handle their sexual differences. For this reason, the remaining methods are geared toward helping you find new ways to approach your sexual difficulties with your spouse. Read them all, and use what appeals to you. But keep in mind that no two people or relationships are exactly alike. What works for someone you read about in this book may not work for you. What works for you may not work for your friend whose sexual relationship needs some help. In fact, what works for you one day, week, or month may not work the next.

Relationship problem solving requires a trial-and-error mind-set. You try something, and then you watch your spouse's reaction carefully. If you get a positive reaction, you know you're on the right track and you keep going. If you get nothing, you might try once more. But if your spouse reacts negatively, quit it. It's as simple as that: you do more of what works, less of what doesn't work. If more people understood this philosophy, I'd be out of business. (And that would be great, by the way. Hawaii sounds pretty good to me right now.)

Because I believe that simplest is best, I have arranged these strategies in order of the most direct or straightforward to the most complex. As a general rule, I would advise you to work these methods top down. However, another one of my basic philosophies is that you have to be genuine in your approach to things in life, so if a particular strategy doesn't feel right for you, skip over it. You are the expert in your life, not me. Take what makes sense to you here, and leave the rest.

Keep two more things in mind as you read the specific techniques. Remember that patience isn't a virtue; it's a necessity. If you and your spouse have been distant for a while, the kind of change you're hoping for may take a while. Big changes won't occur overnight. Don't become impatient and revert to your old ways just when you're getting started. Stay the course, and have faith that things will improve eventually. Second, try not to take your spouse's feelings about sex personally. If you read Chapter 3, you know that your spouse's interest in sex may or may not have anything to do with you. The calmer and more loving you can be with your spouse, the more likely s/he will respond positively. I know it's incredibly hard not to be reactive, but regardless of what you're feeling, you need to remember that you always have a choice as to how you behave. Feelings come and go. You can choose to allow your feelings to push buttons, or you can choose to be more mindful in your response.

If things don't go exactly the way you wish and you find yourself in a heated moment, rather than shoot from the hip, take a deep breath and ask yourself, "What am I hoping to accomplish here? Is what I'm about to do or say going to bring me closer to that goal or push me away?" If your actions are going to push you away from your target (which I presume is more closeness), then don't do it. Regardless of what you're feeling, don't do anything that will alienate you from your spouse. You've done enough of that already. Do what works. And speaking of what works, how about those solutions now?

BREAKTHROUGH SOLUTIONS

Time Together—Testosterone for the Soul

By now, you already know that your spouse might need to feel close emotionally in order to desire you physically. And you're probably well aware of the infamous catch-22—that many people feel just the opposite: a satisfying sexual relationship is the first step in feeling close. You may be one of those people.

If you read the section of this book that's devoted to your spouse, you know that I advised him or her to pay more attention to your sexual relationship even if s/he is not feeling particularly close to you at the moment. In other words, I asked your spouse to stretch beyond his or her comfort zone. I knew you would appreciate that.

But now it's your turn. If you want your sexual relationship to improve and want your spouse to feel more excitement and passion, you are going to have to make a concerted effort to understand the importance of intimacy from your spouse's perspective. And by intimacy, I mean emotional closeness, friendship, and camaraderie. I mean caring, tenderness, and sharing. I mean communicating on a deep personal level, bearing your innermost thoughts. And nothing, absolutely nothing, substitutes for the importance of spending quality time together.

Your spouse needs to feel important to you—more important than work, kids, hobbies, extended family, friends, community commitments. Your spouse must feel as if s/he is numero uno. You need to put aside other things you do to make time for your marriage, to be together. Even if you are a two-career family, and many of us are these days, you need time away from the children—just the two of you. Leave the cell phones at home. Trash your pager. Hold your calls. Postpone your projects. Turn off your television at home. Look into each other's eyes and talk. Talk about yourself. Ask about your partner. Find out what s/he is thinking and feeling. Laugh about the past. Dream about the future. There is no greater aphrodisiac for your spouse than the formula above. It's testosterone for the soul.

Based on your lack of physical closeness, I wouldn't be surprised if you're not exactly in the mood to be Mister or Ms. Nice Guy/Gal right now. That's okay. You don't have to be in the mood; you just have to do it. Read Chapter 2 where I talk about real giving—when you give to your spouse the things your spouse wants and needs whether you understand or agree with them or not, whether you're in the mood to do it or not. You do it because you love your spouse and because love is contagious. One good deed begets another and another and so on.

If you want your spouse's passion to reemerge, you've got to bring more intimacy into your marriage. Don't wait for your spouse to change. You change. Keep in mind that intimacy is foreplay.

The Hallmark™ Solution

Some people tell me that they're not interested in sex because their spouses aren't romantic. For them, sexual desire is strongly linked to feeling courted, appreciated, and sexually attractive. Romantic people love when their spouses plan intimate activities with painstaking care or lavish them with thoughtful gifts on birthdays, holidays or, for that matter, on just about any day. They melt when reservations are made at new restaurants and the child care is prearranged. They adore unusual surprises, Hallmark™ cards, candlelit bubble baths, and frequent "I love you's." And unless die-hard romantics receive the kind of attention they need, their libido goes limp.

If you're married to someone who fits this description, you know who you are. You've heard not once, but many times, about the importance of romantic overtures. You've been chastised about missed events, the wrong cologne, or the ill-phrased expression of love. And if you are about as unromantic as a person gets, you have had an impossible time understanding your spouse's needs. In fact, you might even think s/he is superficial or sickeningly sentimental. But if you want to seduce your spouse or bring back the passion, you really don't have to feel the same way your spouse does on this matter; you just have to do romantic things. Your gestures will be appreciated even if they're not your thing. Let me give you an example.

Jerry and Nicki were having serious problems in their marriage, a second marriage for both of them. Jerry had two daughters from his previous marriage, and Nicki had one son, Brad. Nicki's first husband had died when Brad was seven years old, and she was eager to remarry to provide Brad with a father. Jerry was crazy about Nicki, and their marriage was very loving, romantic, and sexually alive. However, despite their love for each other, Jerry had convinced himself that bonding with a male child was not something he was able to do. He just wasn't comfortable relating to Brad. Over the years, Jerry's unwillingness to foster this father-son bond led to Nicki's growing resentment. When I met them, her hurt and frustration about the lack of connection between Brad and Jerry made her lose all of her sexual desire for him. They had stopped making love.

I decided to meet with Nicki alone. Nicki told me that when she met Jerry, he was the answer to her prayers. He seemed like the most romantic, affectionate man she had ever met. She envisioned how his love, sincerity, and gentleness would be wonderful attributes for a father figure for her son. Initially, Jerry seemed comfortable with Brad, but as the years progressed, their relationship never flourished; they rarely talked, and Jerry showed little interest in Brad's activities. As a result, the very thing that fueled Nicki's desire for Jerry—her appreciation of his nurturing side—had died. She was strongly considering divorce and had contacted an attorney.

When I met alone with Jerry, he confessed to not understanding why Nicki placed so much importance on his developing a good relationship with her son. He thought his romantic gestures—getting her roses each year on the anniversary of the day they met, arranging exotic getaways, being expressive verbally about his profound love and attraction for her—should have been enough to keep them connected. But he was wrong. Nicki's definition of romanticism was somewhat broader. Her knight in white armor was the protective, loving father figure to her son. That's what turned Nicki on. I told Jerry that although he was a romantic guy, he had been missing the mark, and if he truly wanted to win back his wife and restore her passion, he'd have to be romantic, "Nicki style"; he'd have to put more effort into relating to her son. He understood and agreed.

Two weeks later, a bubbly and considerably happier appearing Nicki entered my office. She could not believe the changes in her home. She thought a miracle had happened. Jerry and Brad were becoming buddies;

they were talking more, watching sports on TV, and doing outside chores together. Nicki couldn't have been more thrilled. And her excitement about their blossoming relationship had immediately spilled over into their love life. Nicki told me, "It's really strange. I've been feeling so much more sexual lately. We secretly meet at home over lunch to have a little rendezvous, or the kids will be wondering why mom and dad are in the bedroom at three o'clock in the afternoon with the door locked!"

Although the changes in Nicki's sexual desire might have been a mystery to her, they weren't to me. Jerry courted her in the manner in which she needed to be courted, and she responded passionately, both emotionally and physically.

NAG BUSTING: A TECHNIQUE FOR WOMEN

When I met William, he told me that his sexual desire for his wife, Mary, was nonexistent. "She's always angry and critical. She's constantly telling me what I do wrong or how I've fallen short of her expectations," he said. Mary's criticisms came at a time when William was already struggling with feelings of self-doubt; he had been laid off from work six months prior. His ego was deflated. During the six months that William was unsuccessful at finding gainful employment, he did a great deal of housework and helped with their children. He wished his wife would show more appreciation for his contribution to his family and be more supportive of his raw emotional state. But Mary's frustration with the drop in his libido and his failure to provide for their family prevented her from approaching William more lovingly. William told Mary, "When you're nasty to me, I just want to be away from you. I can't understand how you can pick on me and then expect me to want to be physical with you. It's just not going to happen."

Eventually, I helped Mary recognize William's pain over his job loss. She also began to see how her criticisms pushed William away. She decided to employ a kinder, more compassionate approach. She let William know she understood how hard it must be to have been let go from his job. She made more of an effort to boost his ego by complimenting him about his efforts to help in whatever way he could. She discovered that kindness boosted not only William's ego but also his libido. And she discovered yet another benefit of nag busting; as it turned out, a self-confident, sexually satisfied man is a much more impressive job applicant as well. Four weeks later, he landed a job.

In the years I've worked with couples, I've heard many, many men say that they get turned off when their wives are critical or nag. They lose their desire to be close. Many of these men have difficulty getting or maintaining erections.

Have you been bossy recently? Critical and nitpicky? Have you told yourself, "If I don't manage things, who will?" You need to know that it's hard for a man to feel manly if you berate him or tell him what to do much of the time. Some men fight back or let negative comments roll off their backs when their wives are pushy or demanding. But other men take their wives' critical comments to heart, and it flattens any sexual desire on the spot. They feel demoralized, not sexy.

My husband has complained that I tried to control everything in our marriage and that I drove him away. I admittedly did try to control and organize much in our hectic lives. I now hope that changes I have made during our separation will ultimately create a more comfortable and safe environment for him. I'm hoping that greater sexual intimacy will evolve between us soon.

You need to take an honest look at yourself. Even if you think the things you complain about are legitimate, you must begin to see the connection between your unhappy attitude and your husband's disinterest in sex. And even if your unhappy attitude is *because* of your husband's disinterest in sex, you need to stop being negative and start being nicer—even if you don't feel like it.

Just a few weeks ago, I was ready to walk away from my marriage. My husband's attitude stunk. He thought *I* should do everything around the house, and he could relax and do nothing. We fought every other day and started to not like being around each other. I have nagged and waited ten years for just a tad of help around the house. I never wanted him to be a maid and scrub toilets, just a little helping hand now and then . . . It happened.

Several weeks ago, I came home for lunch. He had the day off, and the house was clean—dishes done, all the clutter picked up!!! I almost thought I walked into the wrong house. I about died. I was walking on air. Why the clean house? I've given this a lot of thought.

I know that I have been more patient with him and made extra efforts to be nice and not bitchy. I've complimented him and let the small things ride. Last night I caught myself three times . . . I was gonna nag him and instead, I let it go. They were little things . . . things not even important enough to mention!

Let me tell you, if these are the results I am going to get, I am never going to nag again! I am so happy about this that I just want to burst. And although our sex life had become almost nonexistent, in the last couple of weeks, sex has not only been more intimate and intense, but much more frequent. I am just so happy/thankful. I had to let you know.

P.S. Quick update—For lunch today I made love with my husband, or should I say he made love with me. Then to top it off, I no sooner got back to work than he called me just to say he loves me! I am so happy, I don't know what to do with myself.

———

I am twenty-five. I have been with my husband ten years this October, married for two. About six months ago, things were getting pretty crappy. No abuse—just the typical, "I do everything, he does nothing. I nag, then he withdraws from me" cycle. I had had enough! I started being nicer to him, and now he helps. He even cleans the house. Our sex life on a scale of 1 to 10 went from a 3 to an 8.5!

———

Perhaps as you're reading this, you're saying to yourself, "I'm not terribly critical. I'm no more negative to my husband than my friends are to theirs." Even if you aren't overly critical or controlling, here's the $64,000 question: Are you complimentary? Do you let your spouse know when he's pleasing you, when he's getting it right?

I once led a discussion group with women who were having difficulties in their marriages. As they complained about their relationships, I asked, "If your husbands were here now and you weren't and I were to ask them, 'Does your wife tend to be critical or complimentary?' what would your husbands say?" Instantly, every woman in the room said, "I'm critical." One woman admitted, "We live on a farm with lots of acreage, and when I came home from work last night, my husband had mowed three acres of grass. And what did I say to him? I pointed to a very small section of grass beneath some trees and said, 'You missed a spot.' Nice, huh?"

Running commentary on what people do wrong doesn't turn everyone off sexually, but it does many people, and your partner may be one of them. So start being kinder, and see if it starts to melt the ice.

If you're a man reading the Nag-Busting Technique, you may see yourself in this section as well. Although the word *nag* is typically used with women, men do their fair share of nagging. (Trust me, they do.) Women call it *controlling*. If any of this has rung true with you, you need to quit complaining and start being nicer, too.

The Housework Solution

Did you notice what women in the previous examples were complaining about? That's right, housework. Show me a woman who feels as if she's doing more than her fair share of housework or child care and I'll show you a woman who has more than her fair share of "headaches." Nothing turns a woman off quite as effectively as the feeling that she's doing most of the work at home. When a frazzled woman tells herself, "I feel as if I'm being taken for granted. There's no real partnership here," I can guarantee that you won't find her burning the midnight oil dreaming up ways to please her husband sexually.

If your wife has been one of those responsibility-ladened people and her requests for more help haven't inspired you to oblige, even if you think she's asking too much, you can't afford *not* to do it. Her resentment for feeling taken for granted will never go away on its own. You need to become more involved at home and show her that you care about and appreciate her. If you don't, it will jeopardize your sexual relationship for sure. Pitching in will definitely get her attention and might make her more open to thinking about your needs. Just remember, when a low-desire woman feels burned out, the first thing to go on her to-do list is sex. Time for some burn-out prevention.

Focus on the Exceptions

During the two decades I've worked with couples, I can safely say that no matter what sorts of problems people experience, no matter how troubled their marriages might be, there are times when things go more smoothly. People tend to take the good times for granted and not pay much attention to them. Conversely, when things go wrong, we don't pay attention to anything but the problem. We analyze it to death. We feel badly about it. We try to assign blame. We talk about it. We dream about it. We become it.

This is unfortunate because when you focus on the problem, you become a "problem expert" but remain a "solution novice." The exciting news is that the answer to most problems lies in knowing what's different about the times when your problem *doesn't* occur. Although most people think that problem-free times are flukes—they just happen—nothing could be further from the truth. When marriages are peaceful, loving, and conflict free, both spouses are doing something differently. They're in their "getting-along" mode. The key to discovering what's different about your getting-along mode is to reflect on times when things go well (when you're having constructive conversations, enjoying each other's company, feel close and connected), and then ask yourself:

What am I doing differently then?
What is my spouse doing differently then?
What are we doing differently as a couple or family?

For example, when the two of you get along better, are you spending more time together and talking more? Are there fewer family obligations? Is work less intense? Are you more willing to overlook small annoyances? Do you call your spouse more frequently? Are family meals more prominent an activity? Are you helping more around the house?

Once you figure out what you and your spouse do differently when you're getting along, start doing that, even if you're not feeling connected at the moment. Focusing on exceptions is a good thing to do in regard to your sexual relationship too. Regardless of how distant you and your spouse have been, chances are there was a time in your marriage when things were more lively and loving. Reflect back to those times and think about what was different about your marriage or your sexual relationship when things were clicking. Were you taking more time for foreplay? Were your work schedules more conducive to lovemaking? Was it B.C. (before children)? Were you more adventurous and lighthearted? Did you put more energy into finding new ways to make your sexual encounters stimulating and creative?

As you answer these questions, you may notice that some of the factors in play in the past are no longer feasible. For example, if your great sex occurred B.C., children are an irreversible decision. However, even if what you've identified is no longer a possibility, elements of that situation still might be. Ask yourself, "What was different about our marriage and sex life before we had children?" Let's say your answer is, "Sex was more spontaneous," or "We weren't so tired," or "Johnny didn't sleep in our bed." (A word about spontaneity after children come into your life: You may not be able to jump each other's bones when the mood strikes. You need to do more planning to make sure you have the privacy you need. But once you get alone, you can be as spontaneous as you desire. Consider it planned spontaneity.)

In regard to the other responses—"We weren't so tired," or "Johnny didn't sleep in our bed"—they offer great clues about what you need to do differently to bring back the spark. If you were feeling less burned out, you would need to sit down together and find ways to cut back on obligations, get help, or do a better job of sharing responsibilities. If better sex happened when Johnny wasn't in bed with you, you'd have to help Johnny find his way back to his own bedroom, where he belongs anyway. Identify what works, and then do it.

Strike While the Iron Is Hot

This method is really another form of focusing on exceptions and doing what works. I have talked about the fact that testosterone levels rise and fall. This is important for you to know because there may be patterns to the times when your spouse is more receptive than others. For example, studies show that in many men, testosterone surges in the early morning, around 7 or 8 A.M. If you're a woman whose husband isn't as interested as you would like, even if you're sleepy or not quite in the mood early in the morning, you might consider giving yourself an extra push to see if your husband is "up" yet. If so, you might as well strike while the iron is hot.

If you're a man, you should know that your wife's testosterone spikes too. It may be later in the evening, in the middle of her menstrual cycle, or closer to the end of the month. Ask your wife to see if she notices differences as to when she feels slightly sexier than others.

Speak Your Mind

Your spouse is not a mind reader. When you're in the mood to be sexual or make love, you need to make sure you're clear and direct about your intentions. Believe it or not, people who think they're crystal clear about their being "in the mood" aren't always so. They often just drop hints or innuendoes that are easy to miss. Tessa is certainly one of those people.

Tessa and Dennis sought my help because they thought they were growing apart. They had been married for five years. Tessa explained that although she knew when they got married that she was more interested in sex than Dennis was, she valued so many other aspects of their relationship that she assumed she could just accept their sexual differences. A year into their marriage, she began wondering if she had made a mistake.

Tessa said, "I'm always the one who wants to make love, and now Dennis never does. This isn't what marriage is supposed to be about." As the conversation unfolded, it became clear that although Tessa thought she was very forthcoming about her sexual desires, she really wasn't. And when Dennis didn't detect her hints, she took it personally.

Dennis was confused by Tessa's description of their marriage. Although he knew she was "hotter" than he, to his recollection, she hadn't been initiating sex recently. He thought she was cooling down. Dennis asked Tessa, "When was the last time you approached me?" She said, "Last night. Don't you remember? Right before we went to bed, I asked you if you were tired and you said yes." Dennis turned to Tessa and said, "I was tired, but you didn't express any interest in making love. You asked me if I was tired."

Tessa replied, "What do you think I was talking about when I asked you that?" Dennis told her, "I thought you wanted to know if I was tired." Get the picture? Dennis had missed the fact that Tessa was testing the waters, and understandably so. Hinting leaves too much room for misunderstanding.

You need to make sure that when you're interested in being intimate with your spouse, you're making yourself perfectly clear. This isn't to say that you always have to spell things out verbally. In some marriages, other overtures work better. For example, some people like the hands-on approach. Others prefer suggestive nonverbal signals or actions. Think back to times when your spouse was most receptive. What worked then? Use the invitation most likely to prompt your spouse to want to join your party. Just make sure your message is received.

If you haven't told your spouse your feelings about your sexual relationship in general, you need to do that too. Many people just sweep things under the carpet until they feel so bad they have an affair or leave the marriage.

All my friends said their sex lives went out the window after kids came. I figured it is just a normal side effect of having kids! So I guess I accepted it, but he did not. But whenever I would try to talk to him about it, he would brush me off, and he never told me that it bothered him. I thought that he also accepted it as a natural side effect. Then he started working a second job, and eventually I found out he was having an affair. One day he came home and told me the marriage was over. He was going to live with her. I was willing to work on things in any way necessary. I'd go to a therapist. I'd do anything to save our marriage. But his solution was just to leave!

But the thing that I find truly sad is that at the point when he said he had decided to leave (with no prior discussion), both of our kids had successfully completed sleepovers at friends, and I had a renewed sense of hope that now my husband and I could escape for those occasional romantic bed and breakfast excursions that we had enjoyed so much pre-kids. The window of opportunity for us to have moments of privacy had just increased, but my hope was pointless because he had already turned to another!

Maybe you're not one to brush things under the carpet; you've discussed your feelings with your spouse. But you still might not have spoken in a way that s/he could hear. You might not have been clear enough. Although it's important your spouse knows of your discontent, it's more important that you explain what you'd like to see changed. Talk about tomorrow rather than the past. And be specific! It will help to review the goals you set earlier in this chapter and share those thoughts with your spouse. Talk in action-oriented terms.

Since this is such a sensitive subject, you have to set a conciliatory tone for your conversation by opening with positive thoughts: "I would like to talk with you. I really love you and want to be closer to you. When we aren't close physically, I don't feel connected to you. I'd like for us to change that. I would really like it if you would _____ [fill in the blank with your goals]." Here are a few more suggestions of how to approach your spouse about your feelings so you can be heard.

Use the "F" Word: A Suggestion for Men

When I say use the "f" word, it may not be what you're thinking. "F" stands for feelings. If you read the section geared toward your wife, you will have learned that she might be totally in the dark about what you're going through right now. She might believe in her heart of hearts that the only reason you're so interested in sex is that it's a physical release. You just gotta' do it; you're wired that way. And I told your wife that to some extent, she's right. But I also told her that sex means much more to you than that.

I explained that when you touch, hold, kiss, and caress your wife, you feel a sense of closeness and connection. Being physical and intimate draws you near to her and reminds you of your love for her. I also told her that when your sexual relationship breaks down, it makes you feel very despondent. Although she knows you're not happy about the lack of sex, she thinks it's because you're not having orgasms. She doesn't understand how a distant sexual relationship wears on your soul. She doesn't quite get what it does to your self-esteem or your sense of manliness. Your wife is unaware of the depth of your feelings—your sadness, despair, resentment, hurt, confusion, and loneliness.

But in some ways, you can't blame your wife for missing the boat. Most men aren't exactly experts at talking about their feelings. When you read this, you're probably thinking, "I talk about my feelings all the time. I tell her how angry and resentful I am to have to spend my life with someone who doesn't like sex."

Yes, that you do. Men, especially passionate men, are usually fairly skilled at discussing their anger. Although talking about anger and resentment can be productive from time to time, that's not what I am talking about here. Your wife already knows about your anger; she *doesn't* know about your hurt. Since men are raised to be strong and independent, they're not encouraged to discuss their vulnerabilities. They're just supposed to have a stiff upper lip and deal with it. Men don't get their feelings hurt any less often than women; they just deal with it differently . . . mostly by themselves or with anger.

If this sounds familiar, the first strategy that you should try is to let your wife in on all the emotions you have felt and are feeling. Discuss your vulnerabilities. Talk about how much you miss her. Tell her what her touch really means to you. Explain the difference between sexual excitement and the emotional connection you feel. You see, for women, talking about feelings is talking their language, and if you want to get through to a woman, you have to talk in a way that makes sense. You have to talk with your heart.

Most women are caretakers, and they'll be more likely to want to protect and care for you if you show your softer side. When you're angry, you don't appear to need protection, love, or empathy. In the face of anger, women feel they need to take care of and protect *themselves.* So even if you think you've said it all, you probably haven't. You have to try again. Do it with your heart, not your head. Heed this advice (although I included this letter in the section geared to your spouse, I felt it was important for you to read too):

You guys really need to understand how important it is to communicate the hurt and rejection to your wives. It took my husband sixteen years before he finally said it in a way that I understood and I got it. Before that, it was just the same old argument: he wanted more, I wanted less. I know that sometimes I probably was punishing my husband for all the wrongs I felt he inflicted on me. I really didn't see sex as his way of expressing love for me. A lot of times I felt it didn't matter who was in the bed next to him; he just wanted some! Well, when I finally "got it," I did a complete 180 and actually really enjoyed it. I found my own sexuality again as a result.

If you're a woman with higher desire and you're reading this, I know that you have been able to identify with much of what I just wrote. Your husband's rejections have hurt you and made you question yourself and your femininity. You've felt confused and despondent. However, if you're like most other women, you've probably done a somewhat better job at discussing your hurt and sense of rejection. Women are raised to believe that talking about feelings is an acceptable thing to do. However, not all women fit this mold. If you think that your anger rather than your hurt has been the primary emotion voiced in your conversations about sex, you should try using the "F" word too. Be softer, kinder, and more vulnerable. See what happens.

If you've tried telling your spouse what you need in a nonjudgmental, loving way and it hasn't worked, you should consider the next suggestion.

Good Things Come in Smart Packages

Years ago, I worked a great deal with adolescents and their families. I remember countless cases when the parents wanted their kids to do certain things but the kids absolutely refused. And then their parents would insist, offering reasons the kids should comply: "You'll learn good study habits," or "It will make you a stronger person," or "That's what I had to do when I was a kid." But the explanations weren't compelling enough, and nothing ever changed. After repeat offenses, the kids would get punished. No amount of reasoning with them made a difference. The kids thought they were right, and they weren't going to change. Never mind that they were losing privileges left and right.

When I approached things a little differently, I got better results. Sometimes I would get the kids alone and tell them, "It really must be a pain in the butt to have your parents breathing down your neck all the time and telling you what to do. You must hate it when they punish you." My words were music to their ears. Then I would wonder out loud, "Gee, I wonder what you would need to do to get your parents off your back?" "That's easy," they would tell me; "I would just have to _____ [come home on time, make my bed, do my homework, and so on]"—the same behaviors their parents were expecting. Although unimpressed with the reasons their parents offered them for following the rules, they liked the idea of getting their parents to back off. Together, we would then scheme how they might "underhandedly" shock their parents by doing the things that would get their parents to back off. Sneaky, eh?

The obvious moral to the story is that even if you have the most incredible suggestion in the world, you might not be able to convince others of your brilliance if you don't approach them in a way that makes sense to *them*. You have to appeal to *their* way of thinking, not yours.

So what does this mean for you? You need to review the way in which you've been approaching your spouse about improving your sexual relationship. You need to think about your packaging. Have you tried to motivate your spouse, a person who prefers a good crossword puzzle to pleasures of the skin, to get help because having a good sex life will feel good physically? Have you been emphasizing how your needs aren't being met to your partner who believes happiness comes from within? Have you been telling your spouse who believes that a good sexual relationship comes not from obligation but love, that part of being a good husband or wife is being a receptive sexual partner? While all of your explanations might make sense to you, they might not click with your spouse. You need to think about what might motivate *him* or *her.*

I know a man whose wife wasn't physical at all, and this bothered him. He yearned for more physical closeness, even nonsexual hugging and kissing. His wife told him that touching feels good, but then for that matter, so does taking a hot bath, and taking a hot bath is a lot easier.

I asked him what he tells his wife about his need for more sexual connection, and he said, "I say, 'I'm unhappy with the way things have been going. I need more affection,' to which she replies, 'So, what? There are things I'm unhappy about too.' " It wasn't until he realized what truly motivated his wife—their children—that he found a more effective way to get through to her.

He thought about the fact that she devoted her entire life to their children. She home-schooled them. She chauffeured, short-order-cooked for them, and tended to all their emotional needs. They were her life. He knew that her own parents had a very loving, affectionate marriage. He also knew how much she appreciated growing up in that atmosphere. And so he said, "Do you want the kids to grow up not seeing any affection? Don't you think it would be better if they saw us hugging and kissing and loving each other?" That planted the necessary seed. The very next day, she agreed to go to a therapist. Good things come in smart packages.

Are you thinking about what lights your spouse's fire when you ask him or her to change? If not, alter your approach, and you'll have a better chance of getting through.

Good Things Come in Gentle Packages

> I made every mistake in the book in regard to how I dealt with his low sex drive. When dealing with men, I wonder if there is a way to handle it without wounding them. Something like this really hits a man where he lives.

If your spouse feels shame or embarrassment about his or her lack of interest in sex or has low self-esteem or is dealing with a personal problem, you have to be careful how you discuss your concern so as not to hurt your spouse's feelings. This would only compound matters. You may have to pull out your kid gloves. How you address this sensitive issue can make all the difference in the world.

TIMING IS EVERYTHING

The difference between someone really hearing what you're saying or becoming angry and defensive may have everything to do with the timing of your request. Don't broach the subject when you're angry or in the heat of the moment—when your spouse has just declined your advances. Wait until your intense emotion subsides, and things are calm between the two of you. You don't want to say something hurtful that you'll regret later. I know a woman whose husband's desire had waned drastically in recent months. After repeated rejections, she finally got so upset she told him, "If you don't figure out pretty soon, what's wrong with you, I'm outta here"—not exactly a paragon of tact.

TALK ABOUT YOU

Rather than criticize or comment on your spouse's character or actions, talk about how *you* are feeling. For instance, instead of saying, "You're just saying no to punish me," or "You're being _____ [hurtful, insensitive, controlling] intentionally," say, "I know you aren't trying to hurt me, but when we make love so infrequently, I feel as if you're not attracted to me anymore or that you don't love me." When you share your feelings rather than accuse, you're more likely to be met with compassion or sympathy rather than defensiveness.

SHOW EMPATHY

If you want to short-circuit your spouse defending his or her actions, make sure your spouse knows you recognize that your sexual differences are wearing on him or her too. If your spouse believes that you have some sense of what it might be like to be in his or her shoes, s/he won't feel the need to explain things repeatedly. Your spouse might be more willing to approach this issue as a team rather than as opponents. Tell your spouse, "I know this is hard for you too," "I realize that my wanting more physical closeness than you do must be difficult for you at times," or "I can see how upsetting it is to you when we fight about sex." "I know you might feel uncomfortable talking about this because men are 'supposed' to desire sex, but I love you, and I want to be closer to you, so I really want to talk about it."

SHOW A WILLINGNESS TO HELP

Express your willingness to change or approach your sexual relationship differently if it will help in any way. Ask, "Is there something I could do differently that would make you feel more turned on or interested in being closer to me physically?" Make sure your spouse sees you as genuine.

You may not realize it, but sometimes when people are embarrassed to discuss sex, they don't tell their spouses what is bothering them or what they're uncomfortable with sexually. One woman I counseled confided in me about her discomfort with anal sex, but she failed to tell her husband.

> My husband is really into anal sex. Because he wanted to do it, I tried it a few times, but I disliked it. It was a real turn-off to my desire to have sex with him. But he always pushed the issue. I think he thought he could seduce me into liking it. We would be having a perfectly enjoyable mutual encounter, and then he would turn things in the other direction and totally turn me off. I just thought he would get the hint that I didn't like it!

Eventually, she started avoiding sex entirely. That's why it's extremely important for you to demonstrate to your spouse that you are really interested in his or her feelings and willing to change what you can to make having a loving sexual relationship a reality. Make sure your spouse feels safe enough to talk to you about his or her feelings. Don't judge. Don't criticize. Just listen.

REASSURE

If other sexual problems such as erectile difficulties, ejaculation problems, or trouble achieving orgasm are at the root of your partner's low desire, ultimately, it is a good idea to seek professional help with a sex therapist. Your spouse might balk at the idea of talking to a stranger about such a personal issue. If so, you should do the legwork and get the name of a good sex therapist in your area.

You need to put your frustration with your sexual relationship aside to be reassuring to your spouse. Tell your spouse how much you love him or her in spite of your challenges. Take the pressure off by reminding your spouse that a good sexual relationship isn't synonymous with intercourse and orgasms and that you're happy to find other ways to pleasure each other and stay connected physically. Worry interferes with arousal, so anything you can say that will relax your spouse will be helpful. Again, a qualified sex therapist can help you determine the best ways to approach your spouse. For a referral, contact the American Association of Sex Educators, Counselors and Therapists: P.O. Box 5488, Richmond, VA 23220-0488, http://aasect.org. Call 804-644-3288 to schedule an appointment, and even if your spouse won't go, go by yourself. The therapist can give you tools to be helpful to your spouse.

Help Your Spouse Feel Ready

Do you ever feel that your spouse won't make love or be sexual until a long list of prerequisites have been met (Love, 2001)? Are you somewhat bitter because when you've tried to meet your spouse's demands or requests in the past, it hasn't always resulted in his or her being sexual?

While your spouse's prerequisites may feel as if they're a moving target, you need to approach this matter with a new attitude in the future if you want things to change. If every time your spouse tells you what s/he needs to be more sexual you dismiss it, your spouse will feel misunderstood and disregarded. I understand your skepticism, but you have to give your spouse the benefit of the doubt. Don't be cynical. Don't judge. Do what your spouse asks, even if you're not 100 percent sure it will make a difference. Do it anyway.

Nan and David, both in their early thirties, had been married for seven years when I met them. David was moving up the corporate ladder in his company and spent long hours at work. When he was home, he often spent time on the computer or making business calls. Nan felt that their marriage was suffering. She felt that David had lost interest in their sexual relationship, a very important part of their early marriage. Nan described their sexual relationship as having been incredibly passionate. Now, they argued a great deal about sex. Nan felt that David was always coming up with excuses to avoid intimacy. Listen in on a conversation that took place in my office.

DAVID: I've told you before, if you want to make love, you need to approach me right after dinner instead of late at night.

NAN: Yeah, right, you're always on the computer.

DAVID: I told you, just come over to me and tell me you're interested.

NAN: I've done that and you say, "In five minutes, just give me five more minutes."

DAVID: You just need to give me time to wrap things up.

NAN: I'm tired of chasing you. I'm sick of it. Plus, even if I give you time, you're not always up for it. Sometimes you tell me, "The kids are still awake," or "There are things you and I need to talk about first." I always feel you have a list of excuses not to be with me. If you don't want to make love, don't. But stop leading me on.

DAVID: I'm not leading you on. Just because you can drop everything instantly doesn't mean I can. I'm not that way. Sorry.

NAN: Forget it, you're not interested. Why should I always be the one who's pursuing you? See, Michele, this is what I mean. He's not available to me anymore.

I totally understood why Nan's feelings were hurt. Nan wanted David to want her more. It seemed to her that other things always took precedence. But David wasn't disinterested; it just took some work for him to feel relaxed. If Nan were able to take David's requests at face value rather than see them as excuses to avoid sex, she could have David in her arms more often. And although he might be slow to get started, it says nothing about his level of enthusiasm once they dealt with his issues and closed their bedroom door.

After talking to David for a while about Nan's need to have him ravish her once in a while, I switched gears and encouraged Nan to honor David's requests. "If David says, 'Let's wait until the kids go to sleep,' wait until the kids go to sleep. In fact, put them to bed. Take David at his word." Although I could see the hesistant look on her face, she said, "Okay, I will."

A week later, they returned, excited by two things that had happened. One night David was at his computer when Nan expressed interest in making love. As usual, David told Nan to give him a few more minutes. This time, rather than assume that he really wasn't interested, she went into the kitchen, looked at the clock, and timed him. Five minutes later, she walked into his office with a big smile on her face, swiveled his desk chair around, and promptly sat on his lap. He started to laugh, shut down his computer, and joined Nan on a trip to their bedroom. Later that week, David initiated sex for the first time in several months.

Truth be told, there certainly were times in their marriage when, no matter what Nan did, David wasn't really up for having sex. But since, as she learned, that wasn't always the case, Nan opted not to react defensively when David expressed a reason he wasn't quite ready.

Has your spouse ever told you what would make sex more appealing for him or her? Has s/he said things like, "I'd be more interested in having sex with you if _____ [the kids were asleep, you were nicer to me, it weren't so late, the room were darker, the dog was let out, we didn't have to get up so early tomorrow, you took a shower first, you lost weight]"? Have there been times when "everything was in order" but nothing happened? Has this jaundiced you to being willing to do what your spouse has asked for? If so, rethink your position. Show your willingness to create the kind of atmosphere that will help your spouse relax and enjoy being with you sexually.

The Medium Is the Message

People have different learning styles. Some are visual learners; they process information best when they see things. Others are auditory learners; they learn best by hearing information. Still others are kinesthetic learners; they learn best through touching or action. Yet when relationships break down, most relationship experts usually tell you to improve your verbal communication skills. There's nothing wrong with learning how to talk and listen more effectively, but if you really want to be a good communicator and send clear messages, you've got to know something about the person receiving the message. You've got to know his or her preferred learning style. For example, people often say, "I talk until I'm blue in the face," or "If I've said it once, I've said it a million times." When this happens, I suspect that their "deaf" spouses might not be auditory learners. So I often suggest that they write a note or a letter, or take some action rather than keep talking. Frequently this works like a charm.

Barbara was about to leave her marriage of twenty years. Her husband, Martin, was an alcoholic. Although he thought he drank too much at times, he never really did anything substantive about it. Now that their children had all left their home, Barbara wanted to focus on her own life rather than Martin's problems. When she told her grown children about her decision, they urged her to try to work things out and keep the family together. Although she felt fairly certain nothing would ever change, she promised her children she would wait a little longer before contacting an attorney.

In the meantime, although she was convinced she had tried everything, she decided to write her husband a letter explaining her feelings of desperation and her plan to leave their marriage and left the letter on top of their bedroom dresser. Later that evening, she returned home from shopping, and Martin was sitting in their family room. He asked her to sit down and talk with him. Tearfully, he apologized for all the hurt he had caused, admitted that he had a drinking problem, and agreed to quit drinking entirely and attend Alcoholics Anonymous. This was the first time in their lives together that Martin had expressed a willingness to face his drinking demon and do something about the problem. Barbara was extremely surprised at Martin's reaction and his willingness to work on himself. Although she was uncertain about Martin's determination to stick with his plan, she decided to give him a chance.

I have learned from people like Barbara that when frustrated spouses say, "I've tried everything," what they're usually saying is, "I've said everything." If your spouse hasn't been listening to your pleas for more sexual closeness, no matter how you say something, you won't be heard. If you really want to get through to a person who isn't listening with his or her ears, you need to be more creative. Write a letter, leave a sticky note, mark something on a calendar, or take an action. (I know a woman who, after a year of asking her husband to fix the stairs on their deck, got out his toolkit and started doing it herself. Within two minutes, he was right behind her, correcting her and telling her, "Move away, I'll do it.") Get the message?

Another way to think about the medium is the message technique. Couples often tell me that when they can't resolve issues face-to-face, they have more success talking on the telephone. Car phones and cell phones have saved many a marriage in this way. (This is often true in my own marriage, and I have a theory about why telephone conversations work. When you state your point of view, you can't see your spouse's eyes rolling back in his head!) If your conversations with your spouse aren't going anywhere, besides writing a heartfelt letter, try talking on the phone or even e-mailing.

Do a 180

In the previous chapter, I discussed the concept of doing more of the same—that continuing to do what isn't working doesn't work. When you and your spouse argue a lot, it will deaden your spouse's already dull sex drive. So you need to find creative ways to resolve these desire-deadening differences. Doing a 180 is a creative method that will help you improve many aspects of your marriage.

Think about where you and your spouse get stuck. Take stock of what you're doing in those situations, and then promise yourself that the next time you encounter that old situation, you'll do something different. My suggestion is that you do a 180—you change the way you and your spouse interact by doing the exact *opposite* of whatever you've been doing that hasn't been working. One of my favorite examples is something Vicki tried with her husband, John.

Vicki grew up in a family where there was a great deal of conflict, and she vowed that in her own marriage, she would make every effort to have peace. She happened to marry a man, John, who was rather volatile. He had a very low tolerance for frustration.

Throughout their marriage, every time John felt frustrated, he would raise his voice and start "ranting and raving." Vicki's usual response was to rush to his side and try to calm him down. She would reassure him that things weren't as awful as he thought they were. But rather than settle John down, Vicki's reassurances only served to make him angrier and to focus his frustration on her instead. She didn't like that one bit and found herself resenting John quite often.

One day, she overheard John beginning to rumble about something in their home office. As his voice got louder, she headed into the office to see what was going on. She heard him say loudly, "I can't believe my boss expects me to do this! I wasn't at the training. How in the world am I supposed to know what to do?" She felt pulled into the room to comfort him but instead decided to do a 180. She walked over to his desk, loudly and emphatically pounded her fist on the surface several times, and bellowed out, "That's right! What was your boss thinking? If you weren't at that training, you don't know what in the world you're doing. You will never be able to do this project. I can't believe this is happening! It's going to ruin our evening. This is so frustrating!"

There was dead silence. John's jaw dropped. After several exceptionally long moments, John looked at Vicki and said, "Settle down. It will be okay. I'll figure it out." I'm not sure who was more surprised there: Vicki or John. But that's how doing a 180 often works. It kicks the two of you out of automatic pilot. You act differently and trigger a different response in your spouse. Here's another example.

Karla sought my advice about an ongoing parenting conflict with her husband that created distance between them. She thought her husband was too strict, and he thought she was too lenient. Although the details of each argument varied, the pattern always remained the same: she backed the kids; he balked. The more Karla defended her position, the more her husband stood his ground. She found their interactions to be exasperating and hurtful. They would go for days not talking to each other after big fights. Their intimate relationship suffered.

Knowing that those kinds of arguments are often not unlike a tug of war, I envisioned what might happen if Karla let go of her end of the rope. So I said to her, "The next time he brings up the issue of curfew after the school dance [their most recent disagreement], why don't you try something different this time? Why don't you state your view, and if he disagrees, as you suspect, pause for a moment, tell him he's probably right, that he's got a valid point. And then be quiet."

At first, Karla was ready to do battle with *me* because she didn't want to tell her husband that he might be right about his parenting ideas. But I reminded her of what would happen if she told him he was wrong. "Same old, same old," she said, and then agreed to give my idea a whirl.

The next day, her husband raised his concern about their daughter's curfew. After hearing his point of view, she took a deep breath and said, "I suppose you're right. Katie should be home early after the dance. You've got a point there." Not knowing what else to say, her husband ended the conversation, and they both headed off for work. Later that day, her husband called Karla and said, "I've been thinking about it. Maybe we should let Katie hang out with her friends just a little longer. I guess it wouldn't hurt if she came home a bit later." Karla was dumbfounded. It was the first time he had ever loosened the rein. Karla simply replied, "Whatever you think. I'll go along with whatever you want to do." Karla decided on the spot that doing a 180 was going to be on her short list of things to try whenever she and her husband hit a snag.

Perhaps you're thinking that you understand how doing a 180 can break through repetitive relationship habits, but you want to know more specifically how this method might help you improve your sexual relationship. Here's how.

The Seesaw Principle

Relationships are like seesaws: the more one person does, the less the other one does. This simple concept holds true for every aspect of your lives together. If you're the emotional one in the relationship, your spouse is probably more even-keeled. If you take out the garbage all the time, your spouse will be unlikely to do it or even think of doing it. If you handle all social engagements, your spouse will wait for you to tell him or her about the plans you've made rather than make plans. If you do the vast majority of the housework, your spouse will be less inclined to do so.

The second aspect to the seesaw principle is that if you want your spouse to do more of something, you have to do less. So what exactly does this mean for you, and how you should handle your sexual differences? There are a number of ways you should think about applying this concept. Let's go back to the previous chapter, where I described the common more-of-the-same behavior patterns.

Remember the Diagnosis Debate? More of the same behavior? Do you find yourself frequently asking your partner, "What's wrong?" or arguing about who's to blame for your sexual problems or debating the real, underlying cause of your spouse's low desire? Are you the one to nag or remind your spouse to schedule a doctor's appointment, read a book on sexuality, or think about seeing a sex therapist? If your behavior isn't paying off—if it isn't prompting your spouse to do as you suggested—you're probably making matters worse. Your spouse will want to avoid you and your irritating comments. Is that what you really want?

Since you're always the one to take the lead in your sexual relationship—you're the primary fixer and initiator—you are actually allowing your spouse to take a back seat. You're doing all the work. Your spouse doesn't have to do much at all. You've gotten in roles; you're the sexual one, your spouse isn't. The more energy you put into this aspect of your marriage, the less that is required of your spouse.

It's time for you to try something different; resign from the role of fixer/initiator for a while. Back off, and give your spouse some space. Give him or her a chance to miss you and perhaps even feel a bit more sexual without being prodded by you. Sometimes the lower-sexed spouse simply needs more time to allow his or her batteries to recharge. Here's a suggestion. For the next three to four weeks, tell yourself, "I am not going to initiate sexual contact. I won't touch or kiss my spouse in a sexual way. I won't make sexual comments. I won't complain. I won't pout. I will not discuss this plan. I'll just wait to see what will happen when I give my spouse a little breathing room. Let him or her do some of the work, for a change." Quit trying to change things for a while. Put your home improvement project on hold for a few weeks, and watch what happens.

Besides giving your spouse an opportunity to miss you and perhaps wonder why you're acting differently, you will be arguing a lot less. And it's entirely possible that the peace between you might just lead to your spouse's being more interested in being intimate with you.

I'm warning you that backing off won't be easy, especially if you are feeling turned on. It's also difficult because you have been so focused on your relationship (at least the sexual part of it) that you have probably put your other needs aside. It's hard to just quit cold turkey! But rather than spend time arguing about sex, you should use the time to focus on yourself and find things to do that fulfill you. Go out with friends. Start a new hobby. Join a health club. Go to church or temple. Once s/he sees you focusing on *you* rather than your sex life, s/he might want to be more involved in your life in every way. Here is a letter from someone who piqued her husband's interest when she stopped talking and took action:

> The other night I tried to talk to my husband about my need for conversation, affection, and sex. He rolled his eyes, and the only thing he said was, "Here we go again." I stopped there and said, "I know you don't want to hear this, but I need to tell you that I didn't

get married to live like brother and sister. I want and need sex and I am not happy with the way things are." Then I dropped it. He was quiet and distant.

The next evening, I decided to go out to dinner with a friend of mine—a girls' night out. When I got home, he was very attentive. We talked for a while (not about sex), and he was very affectionate and we made love. I think that going about my business and not trying to discuss sex with him anymore made him wonder what I was thinking and made him more interested.

No Private Parts

I enjoy cuddling. He never wants to cuddle or "make out." Sometimes all I want is a little affection, and I definitely resent that the slightest show of affection has to lead to sex. Why can't affection just be shown for affection's sake?

One thing that we did do for a while is have joint bubble baths with candles and nice music. It was very nice. We would both relax and talk to each other. However, eventually one thing would lead to another, and then I started to feel like, "Gee, every time he asks me to have a bubble bath, does that mean he wants sex?" Sometimes I just want to relax and talk—nothing else!

A complaint that many low-desire spouses have is that their spouses, namely you, are not capable of or willing to touch in ways that are simply affectionate but not sexual. They feel that sex is always imminent, that it's impossible to hug, kiss, or even pass in the hall without your wanting more. A peck on the cheek turns to a tongue-thrusting French kiss. A platonic hug leads to hands groping over buttocks or breasts. "Making out" is a means to an end, not an end itself.

Your spouse may be the sort of person who really enjoys touching, hugging, holding, and caressing but since you have other things on your mind, rarely feels that you're honoring his or her feelings. As a result, when you want more, s/he retreats. Eventually, it becomes second nature for your spouse to pull back every time you touch him or her.

If this is true in your marriage, try an experiment. Be affectionate without expecting to become sexual. Hug warmly, and leave it at that. Force yourself to avoid touching your spouse's genitals. Offer to give backrubs for no other reason than just to give a back rub. Novel idea, eh? Your spouse may appreciate your willingness to see things from his or her perspective and become more interested in you and in pleasing you. It's certainly worth a try.

Beauty Is in the Eye of the Beholder

> My wife is eighty pounds heavier than when we met in college. I am roughly the same weight and keep in good shape. My desire for sex with her is nearly gone. I have always been faithful, but recognizing that sex has always been a key to intimacy for me, I now find myself not as interested as I should be in improving either the communication or our sex life.
>
> I have never confronted her with her weight. She has tried occasionally to lose, but I think has now accepted her obesity, and that really turns me off. I feel shallow about this hang-up and have tried to rise above it, but my lack of respect for her attitude and my disinterest won't go away.

You may think it unfair or flat-out wrong, but many people lose interest in their spouses when their spouses stop caring about themselves, their health, their appearance, and their level of fitness. I've had lots of people in my practice say, "After the kids were born, she just let herself go. I'm turned off by her extra weight," or "He sits in front of his computer all day and eats poorly. No wonder he's out of shape. He's not the same man I married," or "I'm sorry, I can't stand _____ [his breath, her cigarette smoking, the way he dresses, her sloppy appearance]. I just don't feel desire anymore."

If your spouse's lack of interest in sex is due to not feeling attraction to you right now, you might be thinking, "How shallow! If my spouse doesn't love me for who I am, for the person inside, then I don't care about him or her either." But the truth is, you do care. You want to feel closer to your spouse sexually. Physical attraction is not a logical thing. People feel it, or they don't. If what your spouse says about your level of fitness, health, cleanliness habits, or appearance has some validity, if you want the relationship to become more sexual, you have to change. Even if you think it's unfair or petty, you still have to change. Staying fit and healthy is important. It's a gift you should give yourself, regardless of what your spouse thinks.

Gladys and Sean had been married for twenty-four years and had three grown children. Their youngest son had just left home for college. Like many other empty nesters, Gladys and Sean were beginning a new phase in their lives together. When Gladys took stock of the state of their marriage, she wasn't very happy. She felt they had very little in common. They rarely went out on dates together and shared very little. But the thing that bothered Gladys the most was Sean's extensive hours surfing the Internet. She had discovered that he was visiting pornography sites and had acquired several e-mail accounts. Gladys was worried that Sean was involved in cybersexual activities. Sean was not willing to attend counseling.

Gladys had already confronted Sean about his behavior, but he saw nothing wrong with his visits to sexually explicit web sites. And when she confronted him about his e-mail accounts, he denied any "foul play." "You're welcome to take a look at what I do with those accounts if you wish," he told her.

Although we discussed her feelings about his on-line activity more extensively, Gladys admitted that their sex life had been practically nonexistent for four years. I asked her why she thought this was so. She told me that her husband mentioned he was unhappy about her allowing herself to get out of shape. She said, "I'll be damned if I go on a diet just because of that!" but as our conversation unfolded, Gladys admitted to being unhappy about her size regardless of her husband's feelings. In fact, at the end of the session, she admitted that prior to our first session, she had already started a new diet and a regime of daily walking. She had lost five pounds.

I congratulated her on her accomplishments and on her decision to get back into shape. I reminded her that substantial weight loss doesn't happen overnight and that she might not get kudos from her husband at first. I urged her to keep her spirits up and stay on her plan even if he didn't yet notice the changes.

However, happily, her husband was very much tuned into the fact that she had begun to take better care of herself. He offered to walk with her in the evenings. She was very pleased. And although she wasn't svelte, her self-confidence improved almost immediately. "It just helped to be doing something about this situation," she said. And it wasn't long after that, two weeks to be exact, that she initiated sex, and her husband responded positively—to hear her tell it, very positively in fact.

If you haven't bothered to work on yourself because you feel over-whelmed or you think that your spouse won't even notice, you may be wrong. Just the fact that you're being proactive might make the difference. If, on the other hand, you've tried to improve your health but have given up very quickly, your spouse probably won't be jumping up and down just because you said you're ready to give it another shot. In fact, s/he might be skeptical about your willingness to stay committed to your plan. If so, your spouse won't be cheering you on. You will have to be your own cheer-leader. Or join a weight loss group or a work-out class. You'll have other people rooting for you. Just stay the course. It will be worth it.

The Do-It-Yourself Solution

No matter how much your spouse loves you or wants to please you, s/he might never have the same sex drive as you. Therefore, it's unreasonable for you to expect your spouse to be at your beck and call every time you feel sexual. You need to take responsibility for satisfying your own needs from time to time. In all likelihood, you are already doing this, and you don't need me to tell you to do it. However, you might be feeling resentful about it, and that's not fair. Although it is my hope that your spouse will invest more energy into your sexual relationship, there will still be times when you're ready to roll and s/he isn't. That's normal, and you need to ac-cept it. As long as your spouse is making more of an effort to understand and care for you and your needs, you need to work harder at accepting your differences. And part of this acceptance entails taking care of yourself occasionally and feeling fine about it. This will be easier for you to do once you truly feel your spouse cares about you and your feelings. And hope-fully, if that isn't happening already, it will, very soon.

Variety Is the Spice of Life

Perhaps your sex life has become routine. Boredom is an industrial-strength sexual desire dampener. Even the most highly sexed person can begin to feel ho-hum about sex if it's always the same old thing. If this rings true of your sexual relationship, it might be time for you to try to spice things up a bit. You need to be creative to avoid sexual boredom. Try a new location, rent a hotel room, experiment with new positions, buy new lingerie, rent a sexy video, try a hot bath, candles, and a massage. Cast your inhibitions to the wind.

Kellie complained that she was losing desire because she was having trouble feeling aroused. It took her considerably longer to have an orgasm, and when she did, it wasn't as strong as orgasms had been in the past. She found herself feeling more and more disinterested each time her husband approached her. She wondered if it was because of her age—she was fifty-two—and whether she should consider taking hormone supplements.

Kellie was menopausal, and it was entirely possible that biological causes were at the root of her sexual difficulties and lack of desire. However, I also wondered about the quality of her sexual relationship with her husband. Kellie confessed to feeling bored. Their lovemaking had become routine and unexciting. Because her mind would drift during their sexual encounters, she found it challenging to maintain feelings of arousal.

I suggested that she talk to her husband about her feelings and for them to plan ways to introduce some novelty into their time together. Kellie discussed what had turned her on in the past—dressing up, varied positions and locations in their home—and agreed to start doing that again. When Kellie returned that following week, she reported that she had no problems with arousal. She had had several strong orgasms, just like in the good old days. Apparently, getting out of their sexual rut was just what the doctor ordered.

Accept the Gift of Love

Sometimes as things improve and your spouse is trying to be more caring about your needs, s/he might decide to become intimate with you—have intercourse, engage in oral sex, give you an orgasm but expect nothing in return—even though sex might not be a burning desire. Rather than feel insulted or put off, accept this as a gift of love. In good relationships, people do things for their spouses all the time that may not be exactly what they feel like doing at the moment. That's okay. In fact, that's more than okay. That's great. Remember what I told you about real giving. Real giving is when you give to your partner what your partner wants and needs whether or not you understand it, like it, or agree with it. Allow your spouse to show his or her love by being sexual even if it wasn't his or her favorite thing to do at the moment. Accept the gift and appreciate it. Good marriages are built on this kind of caring.

When I explained this idea to Ralph, a man in his middle fifties and married for thirty years, his immediate response was, "I don't want her to do anything she's not into doing. Sex is only good for me if I know she's excited." I knew I had my work cut out for me. I told him, "Look, I think it's really wonderful that you care about her feelings and that your pleasure is connected to giving her pleasure. That's what love is about. However, what if it makes her feel good to give you pleasure? What if her sex drive will never keep up with yours but she truly wants you to be happy? If you don't make room for that possibility, you're depriving her of pleasure." After a few quiet moments, he agreed.

If All Else Fails, Be Brutally Honest

I've worked with countless couples where one spouse was so dissatisfied with their sexual relationship that eventually s/he decided to have an affair or leave the marriage. You might be thinking of these alternatives too. Affairs and divorce are lousy solutions. Even if an affair satisfies you temporarily (and it might; newness is a great aphrodisiac), it will only create more problems in the long run. Although an affair can serve as a wake-up call to the low-desire spouse, you can't always count on this. Affairs can also destroy your marriage. And even if your marriage survives, the pain an affair causes is immeasurable.

Divorce isn't a good solution either. It destroys families forever. Plus, if you run from your problems rather than work them out, you might find a more sexually compatible spouse, but since no relationship is problem free, you'll find yourself with a new set of problems in no time flat. The grass truly isn't greener on the other side, even if the other side is more sexually active.

However, as the more highly sexed person, you might be at the end of your rope. You might be fantasizing about someone else or about packing your bags and leaving. Before you decide to have an affair or leave, I implore you to make sure your spouse knows in no uncertain terms the seriousness of the situation. Make certain s/he understands what will happen if nothing changes. Don't threaten in the heat of an argument. Don't say nasty things. Don't blame. Don't criticize. Just tell your spouse calmly (or write a letter) that because of the differences in your sexual appetites, you are so unhappy that you are considering doing something you really don't want to do. Spell out what you've been thinking about. Tell your spouse that this is not a threat, but that you are so desperate, you don't know what else to do. Ask your partner one more time to seek help. Then wait and see what happens.

TRY A LITTLE ACCEPTANCE

Although I truly hope that you have found something in the suggestions that has been helpful to you in terms of getting through to your spouse, being the realist that I am, I know that it's possible that your situation hasn't changed significantly. I hope this isn't so, but maybe you and/or your spouse just haven't been able to turn things around and create a more satisfying intimate relationship.

If not, you have a choice to make, and I see three options. One: you can decide to continue being miserable, resenting your spouse for your differences, continuing to fight, and remaining distant. Two: you can leave or have an affair. You already know what I think about that. Three: you can decide to accept what isn't changeable about your marriage. You can deliberately choose to let go of your ideal notion about your sexual relationship. If your marriage is basically a good one other than your sexual relationship, you can tell yourself, "I love my spouse. S/he is a good person. Other than our sexual relationship, our marriage means a lot to me. I'm not going anywhere. I wish things would be different, but I am going to accept him or her the way s/he is. I will not take his or her lack of interest in sex personally. It's about him or her, not me. From now on, I won't make sex an issue between us. I will focus on the strengths in our marriage and work hard at letting go of the rest."

Hard to do? You bet. But it's a viable option nonetheless. You're not a wimp for deciding to accept your situation as is; you are making a very valid choice. Marriages are never perfect; even the great ones have their shortcomings. Find other ways of building closeness and connection. Just decide to let go.

You may think this a strange suggestion coming from someone who believes in the magic of a good sexual relationship, but it's not. I also believe in the magic of marriage. I know how fulfilling a caring, committed relationship can be. I suggest you really think twice before throwing it all away, especially if you have children. Part of the problem in your marriage has been the lack of sexuality. The other part of the problem has been your reaction to it. Your hurt, anger, frustration, and desperation, while completely understandable, have been taking a toll on your life. Even if nothing ever changes, you can decide to react differently—not just your reactions to your spouse, but how you think and feel about your marriage. If you truly believe that your spouse's lack of interest in sex is not about you and may be something s/he would like to change but doesn't feel equipped to do so, it may soften your feelings about things. If you decide to focus on other aspects of your marriage and your life rather than continuing to work overtime on your sexual relationship, it's not a capitulation. You're not weak. You are making a conscious choice to accept your life exactly as it is. That can be an extremely admirable choice. Don't let anyone tell you otherwise.

One last thought: sometimes when people truly let go, and they do so in a genuine and loving way, with time, their spouses begin to feel a tingling inside. There I go again, always thinking.

~IV~

Doing It Together

~

CHAPTER EIGHT

Can We Talk?

Throughout this book, I have emphasized the connection between emotional intimacy and sexual intimacy. If you haven't gotten that yet, you'll definitely have to stay after class! But what is emotional intimacy, and how do two people create it? Although the answer to this question varies depending on the person answering it, the most common response I've heard over the past two decades is that emotional intimacy has something to do with feeling comfortable being yourself and sharing who you are on a very deep level. And although you can do this in a number of ways, one of the most important ways is through intimate discussion. Couples who are struggling in their marriages often cite poor communication as the primary reason. I'm not a bit surprised. The truth is, couples whose love lasts aren't any more similar in terms of backgrounds, interests, or opinions than those whose love fades. However, couples who rise above their differences have better communication skills. They learn how to deal with their diversities. They talk better.

If you and your spouse have a rough time talking about important issues, it probably leaves you feeling unhappy and distant, two feelings that won't exactly inspire you to be physically intimate. Therefore, if you want to feel more connected, if you want to build your friendship, it's essential that you learn better ways to communicate your thoughts and feelings to each other. In this chapter, I am going to share with you some of the tools I share with people in my couples' seminars. I hope you will read this chapter together so that you can begin to integrate the information and put it to use right away.

Here are some tips for having constructive conversations.

- *If you have something you'd like to discuss, ask your spouse if now is a good time. If so, begin. If not, your spouse should arrange a better time, preferably within twenty-four hours.*

I have a cartoon of a knight in full armor, headgear, six-foot spear, and all. The caption below reads, "I'm ready for that talk now."

When an issue arises, one spouse is usually more prepared emotionally to discuss it than the other. A spouse who is tired, upset, or emotionally unprepared can become unnecessarily defensive and angry. If you want to stack the deck in favor of having a positive outcome, you need to make sure your spouse is ready to talk, even if you're chomping at the bit and raring to go. Wait.

- *Start off on a good note.*

Researcher John Gottman tells us that if you start your conversations out on a sour note, even if you temporarily recover from it, you're more likely to end with dissention. Here's what to do instead.

Even though you will be discussing a hot issue, it's important for you to start off on a positive note. This means that you shouldn't criticize or condemn as your opening statement, even if you feel like it. Frame it positively instead. For example, if you've been incredibly angry with your spouse for not spending time with you and the family, instead of charging, "You don't care about the kids and me. You're never home. You're always at work, and when you are home, you're on the phone. I feel like a single parent," say, "I've been thinking about our relationship. When we're together, I feel so good about us. I can think back to the times when we spent more time together as a couple and as a family and those times just mean so much to me. Lately, you've been very busy, and I haven't been feeling very close to you. I miss you."

Here's another example. Instead of saying, "You are so irresponsible with money. You don't care about what happens in the future or whether the kids will have what they need. You just think about you," say, "I want to talk about our financial situation. It makes me feel scared when we're not financially secure. Lately, I've wondered whether you're giving as much thought to this as I am. I'd like to hear your thoughts."

The long and the short of it is that you need to start off nicely. A spouse who doesn't feel attacked will respond more responsibly.

- **Be specific.**

Remember to talk in action-oriented terms. People don't understand what you mean when you say, "You're disrespectful [critical, lazy, insensitive, and so on]." You have to talk action. For example, if you've been angry because your spouse teases you in front of other people and you dislike it, don't say, "I am angry because you're disrespectful and you don't care about my feelings." Say, "When we go out with friends and you tease me in front of them, it hurts my feelings. It seems to me that you do that a lot. I find myself pulling away from you because of it."

Rather than fill your conversation with adjectives, describe the specific behavior that is troubling you. You'll get a lot further because your spouse will get a better idea of what you want and need.

- **Talk about what you want rather than criticize.**

If you want your spouse to change something, rather than angrily accuse him or her, talk about what you'd prefer he'd do instead. You should be a pro at this by now. All you need to do is to refer to the goal-setting section where I had you practice turning complaints into positive requests for change. That's what I'm suggesting you do here. Talk about what you want rather than what you're unhappy about.

If, for example, you aren't feeling close because you find your spouse to be critical and controlling, don't say, "I don't like being around you because you're so controlling and critical," say, "It would mean a great deal to me if you would compliment me once in a while. Your opinion is important to me, and when you say negative things about my decisions, I feel defeated." Instead of saying, "I can't stand it when all you want to do is lie around the house on weekends and veg out," say, "I'd really love it if you'd be willing to go into the city twice a month and try a new restaurant, then go to a movie or a play. I'd be a happy camper." It helps to talk about the future rather than complain about the past.

• Use I-messages.

When you discuss heated issues, as much as possible, it's important for you to take ownership for the way you feel and to realize that the way you see things is just that—the way you see things. it's not a matter of right or wrong; it's just a matter of perspective. If you don't want your spouse to become defensive, talk about how *you* think and feel as opposed to making blanket statements about the way things are or blaming him or her. For instance, instead of saying, "You're a control freak," say, "I feel controlled by you," adding, "when you _____ [fill in the blank with an action-oriented description of his behavior]." Instead of saying, "People just don't treat each other that way," say, "When you raise your voice, it makes me feel intimidated, and I don't like that." When you tell someone how s/he is or how the world is, rather than describe your reactions and feelings, you open the conversation to debate. Steer clear from this as much as possible.

• If things get heated, take time out.

When I ask couples at my seminars whether they can tell when things are starting to go downhill, everyone says, "Yes, absolutely!" And when I ask, "How can you tell? What's going on in your talk that clues you in that your conversation is beginning to deteriorate?" it's amazing how much they know about their talks turning sour. They say things like, "when our voices get louder," "when we start to talk about the past," "when we call names," "when I feel that knot in the pit of my stomach," "when he stops making eye contact with me," and so on. Unproductive arguments don't creep up on people and catch them off-guard. People see them coming for miles.

Rather than just go with the flow, I suggest to couples that once they recognize that they're headed downhill, they stop and agree to take a time-out. They can separate if they wish, take a walk, clear their heads—do whatever is necessary to prevent further escalation. Then, if they desire, they can resume their conversation. The lengths of their breaks should be predetermined.

I also tell couples that when one spouse needs a time-out, the other spouse must honor it. One of the reasons people are hesitant to break is that they fear that their spouses will not be willing to resume the conversation. This isn't fair. If you take a break and one person still wants clo-sure, it's important to resume the conversation. Even if you don't reach a resolution, it's important for both people to have enough time to have their say.

In my practice, I've noticed that many couples take a break from tough conversations. However, they do it in angry ways. One spouse leaves the room or leaves the house, and the other spouse becomes infuriated or feels abandoned. Time-outs aren't bad; they're good. But you have to have a game plan. You have to agree that it makes more sense to take a breather than hurt each other. Then you have to agree to reconvene with a clearer head. The infuriated spouse won't feel angry anymore as long as s/he doesn't feel abandoned.

• *Feelings aren't right or wrong; they just are.*

One of the most common arguments I hear in my office revolves around one spouse's discussing his or her feelings and the other spouse say-ing, "That's not the right way to look at things," or "That's not the way it really is." Boy, watch the sparks fly after that! No one wants to be told that the way you see things or the way you feel is incorrect. Everyone is entitled to his or her feelings. The way you see things is the way you see things. It's not right or wrong; it just is. It's essential that you steer clear from correct-ing your spouse when s/he discusses his or her perspective on things. Just listen. You can disagree, but understand that your opinion is just your opinion. It doesn't make you any more correct.

• *Don't mind-read.*

If correcting your spouse's feelings is a primo button pusher, mind reading is another one. How do you feel when your spouse tells you what you are *really* thinking or meaning when you say something that you wish s/he would take at face value or what's it like for you when your spouse says, "Don't tell me you were going to call. I know you had no intention of calling me last night," or "I could tell you were in a really bad mood when you came home"? Do you just love it? No, not exactly. I bet you get angry. No one likes to be second-guessed. If we wanted to marry the host of the psychic hotline, we would have married him or her.

So, avoid telling your spouse that you know better than him or her what s/he's thinking, feeling, or doing. You'll be on safer ground.

- ### *Leave the past in the past. Stick to the point.*

Conversations deteriorate when the kitchen sink is thrown in. If you want to have a productive talk, choose one or two points you'd like to discuss, and leave it at that. Don't wander; stay focused. Even if what your spouse is talking about reminds you of past injustices, keep your thoughts to yourself if you really want to make headway. Keeping score and dredging up the past are excellent ways to push your conversation into quicksand. If you don't want to sink, stay on track.

- ### *No exaggeration.*

Another way to guarantee detours from a productive conversation is to use the words, *always* and *never,* as in, "You *always* forget to introduce me to your friends," or "You *never* say a kind word to me." When you exaggerate rather than discuss the issues at hand—proper introductions or kindness—your spouse will be reacting to the fact that you're overlooking the fact that *sometimes* s/he gets it right. Your spouse will take issue with your black-and-white thinking. If you don't want that to happen, don't exaggerate. Talk about a specific incident rather than a personality flaw. Even if you feel as if your spouse does something undesirable all the time, you're probably wrong, and besides, it's not the best way to handle things.

- ### *No name calling.*

This is my "No, duh" tip for constructive conversation. It's amazing that I should even feel it necessary to include it; however, I do. When couples get frustrated, they put on their verbal sparring gloves and call each other names. It's very, very difficult to recover when someone has called you a mean-spirited name. Once name calling begins, agree to take a time-out.

- ### *Don't get discouraged if your partner doesn't follow your lead right away.*

Even though you are using new and improved behavior, it doesn't mean that your spouse will respond in kind immediately. You both have months, years, maybe even a lifetime of less-than-effective communication habits to overcome, and change may not come instantly. If your spouse doesn't pick up on the fact that you've turned over a new communication leaf, stay the course. Don't get discouraged and give up. You've probably done that already, and it doesn't work. Eventually, s/he should come around. Just stay focused on the tools you're learning here, and continue to practice them and model them even if your spouse is a slow learner. Eventually, s/he'll come around because you can't argue with yourself.

• *If he's not deaf, he's heard you.*

I wish someone had taught me this in my first year of marriage. I could have prevented tons of heartache had I known it.

When you finally get up the nerve to tell your spouse your innermost thoughts, even if s/he doesn't agree, understand, or acknowledge your point of view, s/he's heard you. Many times during heated conversations, spouses defend themselves rather than acknowledge that their partners have a valid point of view. However, after having had some time to reflect on the conversation alone, it is often the case that people think through things more carefully and start to make changes to please their spouses. They just don't talk about their willingness to compromise or see things in a new light. They just quietly change.

This is important for you to know. Because your spouse isn't saying, "Yes, dear, you're right," or "I can see your point," doesn't mean that s/he isn't going to take your feelings into consideration and change his or her behavior. Remember, if s/he's not deaf, s/he's heard you. Make your point two times. If your spouse doesn't say something indicating s/he's receptive, you need to stop talking. End the conversation. Zip it. But over the next few days, keep your eyes glued on your spouse. Watch for any signs that s/he's thought about what you said and taken your feelings to heart. If s/he has, it's not necessary to draw his or her attention to it; just enjoy it.

• *Agree to disagree.*

It is unrealistic to think that you and your spouse will always find a solution or compromise that you both find acceptable. Sometimes that won't happen. But believe it or not, this doesn't have to create problems in your marriage. You don't need to have a consensus on everything. In fact, you can agree to disagree peacefully.

In order to agree to disagree and to have this agreement feel acceptable, usually both spouses must feel heard. You have to know what your spouse thinks and feels the way s/he does and vice versa. You really have to make an effort to acknowledge your spouse's point of view. You have to be respectful. You don't have to see eye-to-eye, but you have to tell your spouse that from his or her perspective, you can understand why s/he feels the way s/he does. One of the best ways to reach this sort of understanding is through active listening (Markman, Stanley, and Blumberg, 2001).

*   *   *

Although there are many different versions of this kind of communication exercise, I will share with you the version I teach at my seminars. You and your spouse can practice this together. Some people find it too structured; others have found it to be their communication salvation. I suggest that you try it and see how it feels to you. This is how it goes:

Rule One: Discussions should take place only when both partners feel ready. If one person isn't prepared to talk, s/he must suggest another time in the near future for the discussion to occur.

Rule Two: One person has the floor at a time. It is important to begin the discussion on a positive note. Person A speaks for no more than two or three sentences.

Rule Three: Person B is the designated listener. It is the listener's task to make sure the speaker feels understood. The listener should repeat what s/he has heard to confirm it is what the speaker intended. Person B is not to comment or react, just paraphrase Person A's comments back to him or her. Person A then lets Person B know whether what s/he said is accurate. If so, Person A can make additional points. If not, Person A repeats the point to help Person B really hear what is being said. This speaker-listener interaction continues until the Person A's point is made. Then the speaker should ask the listener for feedback.

Rule Four: Person B now has the floor, and Person A becomes the designated listener. Partners can switch roles as often as is necessary to clarify points and feelings.

Here is an example of this exercise in motion:

JENNY: I have been thinking. When you come home at night, you often
spend time on your computer. I miss having evening time with
you. I know you are very busy at work, but I just wish you could
skip your lunch now and then and get your work done at work
so that when you come home, you're more available to me.

TOM: You're saying that you think I should be more efficient at work
and get all of my work done before I get home, right?

JENNY: That's part of what I'm saying, but it's not the whole thing. I'm
telling you that I miss you. We used to spend time together in
the evenings, and I very much enjoyed that. I want to feel that
our relationship is a bigger priority to you.

TOM: Okay, it's not just that you want to me to finish my work over my
lunch hour. The important message I'm getting here is that you
feel as if you're not important to me. You miss spending time
with me. You'd like it if I would plan better so that our relationship is a higher priority.

JENNY: That's exactly right. That's what I'm saying. How do you respond to that?

As simple as that seems on the surface, I'm here to tell you that when
you and your spouse give this a shot, you'll be surprised at how difficult
this exercise really is. That's because when we have conversations with our
spouses, rather than truly listen to what they're saying, much of the time
we're preparing ourselves mentally for what we're going to say next. We're
defending, disagreeing, and critiquing. It takes real skill just to listen and
not react.

In the example, Tom thought Jenny was criticizing his time manage-
ment skills, and he wasn't able to hear Jenny's longing for him. But because he was willing to continue with the exercise, Jenny made sure he
heard her whole message.

When couples practice this skill, they often have great difficulty at first.
They want to stop their spouses and say, "Hey! You're wrong about that,"
or "I can't believe you see it that way!" or "If I just repeat back what you're
saying, you'll think I'm agreeing with you when nothing could be further

from the truth." However, when they force themselves to quiet their minds and listen and reflect back, their spouses feel heard. And when people feel heard, they don't feel the need to keep repeating themselves over and over or attacking. It's a breath of fresh air. Plus, the listener is comforted by the fact that soon will be his or her time to have the floor. Even if this seems awkward to you, try it. You may be surprised how much you like it. The next time you find yourselves falling head-first into your relationship abyss, grab your lifeline. Agree to do active listening.

*   *   *

This chapter should get the two of you talking about important issues in your marriage, and one of the most important areas is your sexual relationship. Why, then, do most people avoid talking about sex? It's the world's most taboo subject. In the next chapter, let's do some taboo busting. Let's talk about sex.

CHAPTER NINE

Sex Talk

Now that you know more about having constructive conversations, it's time to talk about sex. If you'd prefer having a root canal than talking openly about sex, you're not alone. In the years I've been a marriage therapist, it never ceases to amaze me how many people avoid talking about this intimate subject. I've told you before that I've seen couples who've been married for decades, and the thought of discussing their sexual preferences sends shivers up their spines. They don't share what they like about sex. They don't talk about their disappointments. They don't offer instructions or coach each other. And they don't give feedback when their spouses hit the spot. Some people don't even get louder or moan when their spouses are "getting warmer." They never share their fantasies.

People shy away from discussing sex for lots of different reasons. Many are embarrassed, even mortified. It feels far too personal. No one taught us to talk about sex when we were kids. Although sex education is an integral part of most children's education these days, that's not so for many of us who are now adults. When we were kids, schools thought talking about the birds and the bees was our parents' responsibility. But who taught our parents? Certainly not *their* parents. So for the vast majority of people, the word on sex was mum.

Another reason couples don't discuss sex is that we have this crazy notion that our spouses are just supposed to know what pleases us. We shouldn't have to talk about having good sex; it should just happen. But good sex doesn't just happen. Since no two people are alike, no single formula works for everybody. What one person finds arousing and exciting is a pure turn-off to another. If you want your spouse to know how you feel and what you enjoy, you have to tell him or her. Leave mind reading to the soothsayers.

But perhaps you don't feel comfortable guiding your spouse because you're afraid you'll hurt his or her feelings. If you continue to keep your sexual turn-ons a secret, you'll be miserable, and your marriage will falter. But there's no bigger hurt than hearing your spouse say, "I love you, but I'm not in love with you anymore." If you don't keep your passion alive, it will be hard to stay in love over the long haul. So, don't hold back. But use the tips you'll learn in this chapter. They'll really help.

Another reason you might not talk about what turns you on is that you don't really know yourself. Your body is as much a mystery to you as it is to your spouse. If you don't know what gives you pleasure, what makes you feel aroused, what triggers an orgasm, it's time to go back to school. You have to study your body. You need to know what feels good and what leaves you feeling cold. You can't teach your spouse what works for you if you are clueless. You've got to spend some time exploring your body, getting to know yourself intimately. Although some people feel uncomfortable with the idea of self-stimulation, it's important that you push yourself through your discomfort for the purpose of educating yourself. Once you have more information about what it takes for your body to feel excitement and pleasure, you can begin to have more productive conversations about sex with your spouse.

But there are a few things you should keep in mind before you decide to sit down and discuss matters. Much of the advice that I gave in the previous chapter about constructive conversations applies here. Pick a time when you both feel ready to talk. Don't do it when either of you is tired, in a bad mood, or angry at each other or when there are distractions. Make sure you have enough privacy so you don't feel squeamish or nervous about being interrupted or overheard. A safe, comfortable environment is very important.

Before you begin your conversation, you should have a pretty good idea about what you're hoping to accomplish. As you read some of the reasons couples talk about sex, determine what you're hoping to accomplish and review whether what you're planning to discuss will accomplish that end:

> To let their partners know what feels good
> To talk about areas they'd like to improve
> To negotiate differences in sexual interests and preferences
> To talk about aspects of their sexual relationship that aren't comfortable or pleasurable
> To share fantasies
> To correct faulty perceptions
> To share their vulnerabilities
> To request sexual gifts
> To express interest and attraction
> To heighten sexual pleasure
> To be playful

Now, let's review the tips I gave you in the last chapter and see how they apply here.

• *Start off on a good note.*

Since sex is such a sensitive subject, if you and your spouse haven't talked about sex all that much during your marriage, it will help to ease your partner's mind by beginning with the parts of your sexual relationship that you like. For instance, say, "I appreciate that when I suggest that we try new things, you're often willing to experiment. I like that." Or, "When we take lots of time for foreplay, it feels really good to me. I like that you enjoy taking things slowly sometimes too."

• *Talk about what you want rather than criticize.*

Once you have set the tone for a positive conversation, you can begin to discuss things you'd like to improve. As always, it helps to say what you want your spouse to do rather than focus on the things s/he does wrong. This is not to say that you shouldn't let your spouse know about the things s/he does that are uncomfortable or unpleasurable; you should. However, it helps to emphasize what you would prefer to happen instead. It's a matter of degree. For instance, rather than say, "I really don't like the way you stroke my penis," say, "When you touch the underside of my penis near the head, it feels really good. I'd love it if you would do that more often." Or instead of saying, "I don't like your 'Wham-bam, thank you ma'am' style of making love," say, "When we're done making love, I really like it when you hold me in your arms rather than peel away from me so fast. I like feeling close to you."

• *Be specific. Talk in action-oriented terms.*

This is important. If you want to have a satisfying sexual relationship, you have to tell it like it is. You have to be specific and concrete. I can't tell you how many women have told me, "I keep telling my husband that I want to make love, not have sex, but he doesn't have the foggiest idea of what I'm talking about. That's why I think we're mismatched."

There's no way in the world two people will have the same definition of what it means to make love. If you prefer making love but your spouse doesn't get it, you have to spell out what this means, one step at a time. And as you do, you need to stop thinking that your spouse is dense, resistant, or insensitive. He's not; he's just not you.

You need to figure out which of his touches say "tenderness," "closeness," "connectedness," "emotionality," and so on. Do you feel these feelings of warmth when he touches your hair, looks into your eyes, says "I love you" during the heat of passion, gives you little kisses on nongenital parts of your body? It's your responsibility to figure it out and share the news.

Maybe you've been wanting to tell your spouse, "I wish you were more passionate," or "Take more initiative," or "I wish you wouldn't put so much pressure on me to be sexual all the time." Makes sense to you, right? These requests are not good enough, though. You need to be more specific. Let me give you a few examples.

Instead of saying, "I wish you were more passionate," tell your spouse, "It feels great to me when you let me know what pleases you by making more noise or moving around more energetically. I love it when you say dirty things like 'Fuck me.' It really turns me on."

Instead of saying, "Take more initiative," tell your spouse, "It's great when you are the one to ask me to go upstairs to our bedroom or to tell me you're horny. I feel I'm the one to get things going most of the time. And it would also be wonderful if, when we're making love, you took the lead in suggesting new positions or that we try something new like, using oils or giving each other massages."

Instead of saying, "I wish you wouldn't put so much pressure on me to be sexual all the time," say, "It feels as if you're always talking about our sexual relationship. It would really help me if you just gave me some time to get charged up myself. Please don't bring up talk about our sexual relationship for a week or two. Give it a rest. I know sex is important to you and it is to me too, but the more you talk about it, the less I want it. So give me a week or two now and then without letting me know you're ready."

- **Use I-messages.**

As with any other topic in your marriage, it helps if you talk about how you feel rather than comment on your spouse's sexual abilities or techniques. Keep in mind that things that aren't exciting or stimulating for you might be very exciting to someone else. So, talk about you. Here are two examples:

Instead of saying, "You're so goal oriented and impatient. You don't take enough time to help me feel aroused and you expect me to have an orgasm," say, "When we're being sexual and you slow the pace, I really like it. For instance, I seem to need more time for foreplay in order to feel excited. Also, sometimes I just enjoy making out, and I'm satisfied with that. You don't have to worry if I don't have an orgasm. It's fine with me if I don't from time to time. I wish it would be fine with you."

Instead of saying, "Your sexual desire is nonexistent. I don't know what happened to you, but you're not into it anymore," try, "Lately, I've been feeling as if you aren't particularly interested in having sex with me. It makes me wonder if you're feeling okay or if something's wrong. I miss feeling close to you."

- **If things get heated, take a time-out.**

If things get heated in a good way, take a time-out from talking. If things get heated in a bad way, take a time-out too. When you're discussing differences in how you feel about your sexual relationship, you may find yourselves getting angry or defensive or saying the same things over and over. If this happens, agree to stop talking about sex for a while, and go do something else for a while, either together or alone. Plus, you should always keep in mind that it's important not to say anything in the heat of the moment that you'll regret later. People feel vulnerable when it comes to their sexuality. If you say something hurtful, your spouse is likely to remember it and hold a grudge for a long time to come. Be careful and thoughtful. Don't say anything you wouldn't want to hear yourself.

Prolonging an argument because you are trying to win your partner over won't work very well. You need to approach each other with more openness and caring. If you're arguing about sex, you're probably not listening to each other, and this would be a very good time to pull out your active listening skills. Really hear how your spouse feels. Make sure s/he knows that you've heard him or her. Good things happen when people feel heard.

One of the most touching moments I've ever had with couples happened just a few weeks ago. Lanie and Dennis came in with garden-variety marital problems: a hectic lifestyle, a lack of time together, not enough communication, too much sarcasm, and the usual complications that are created when an extrovert and introvert go to social functions together. It wasn't until several sessions into our work together that Lanie began to talk about her lack of sexual desire. It concerned her because she used to look forward to sex with her husband. Now, they made love once every two weeks, and even that was an effort for her. When Lanie talked about her lack of interest in sex, Dennis, a rather talkative man, was unusually quiet. As she pondered all the possible reasons she might not be feeling sexually inspired, Dennis listened on.

Eventually, I turned to him and said, "I know that Lanie is trying to find out why her libido isn't what it used to be, but in the meantime, how are you doing? What's going on with you?" Dennis went on to say, "Lanie is interested only if everything is perfect. And by perfect, I mean absolutely everything has to be in order. Otherwise she just says no. Sometimes I wish she would be more spontaneous or a little more flexible. If we've had a great evening together and we're feeling close, I'm thinking to myself, 'Maybe tonight . . . maybe she'd be willing to make love even though it's not on her schedule.' But it doesn't happen. I just have to wait for her to be in the mood."

I asked Dennis, "What's that like for you when Lanie says no so often?"

And he responded, "It hurts. I feel rejected. I don't feel attractive or wanted by her, and that really hurts my feelings. I try to brush the bad feelings aside, and sometimes I can, but it's really hard because I don't feel good about myself."

Before I could shift gears and ask Lanie what she thought of what Dennis had said, I noticed she was crying. She grabbed Dennis's hand and looked him in the eye and told him, "I feel so bad. Not once, not a single time when I turn you down, do I ever think about *your* feelings. I'm only in touch with what *I'm* feeling at the moment. I never think about you, how you might be reacting or what it's like to be you. Dennis, I am so, so very sorry. I feel terrible." Dennis cried. I cried too.

But I can only speak for myself. My tears were not just of sadness; they were about optimism for the future. I know firsthand what can happen in marriages when spouses really listen to each other. I know how empathy and understanding can transform lives. And in that moment I shared with them, I bet my life that Lanie and Dennis would experience such a transformation in the months that followed. And I'm not a gambling woman.

• *Feelings aren't right or wrong. They just are.*

No matter how divergent your views are about sex, unless you or your spouse is doing something illegal or hurtful, there is no right or wrong way to think or feel about it. Some people really enjoy watching X-rated videos, while others find the thought upsetting. Some people like to play out kinky fantasies, while more inhibited people would find these sexual role plays weird or distasteful. There are few universal rules about satisfying sex. Nonetheless, when you're married to someone who enjoys things you dislike (or vice versa), it creates challenges for your relationship. You need to find ways to compromise, to meet in the middle.

When I do couples' seminars, it often strikes me how rigid couples are when it comes to problem solving. They tend to see things in black or white. It's either my way or his or her way, and they end up feeling angry and distant.

When I listen to their dilemmas, I can almost always see the gray areas. My vision is rarely black and white. Even when people's positions are far apart, I never see them as mutually exclusive. Some solutions or compromises require more creativity than others, but I usually believe that with determination and a little elbow grease, we can find a win-win resolution. Here's an example.

Edie and Roy were married for thirteen years and had two boys. When I asked them what they were hoping to accomplish by coming to my office, Edie said, "I'm not going to beat around the bush. I've been unhappy for a long time. Roy and I haven't made love for two years, and we're here because I just told him I want a divorce. I'm not going to live my life this way anymore. I've given this a lot of thought, and as far as I'm concerned, it's over." Roy looked despondent when she spoke.

"I don't want a divorce," he said, "but I don't think that Edie has tried at all to understand what I'm going through. I've been feeling very depressed for a long time. Depression tends to run in my family. I know I haven't been the greatest husband, but she doesn't make any effort at all to try to see things from my perspective. She just gets angry at me and impatient. She always tells me, 'If you're so depressed, get over it, do something. I'm tired of living like this.' I can't just snap out of it the way she thinks I can. And I don't want to take medication." Roy then turned to Edie and asked, "Do you think *I* like living like this?" Turning back to me he added, "And yes, I admit it, I just don't think about sex. Ever."

Edie and Roy were both so emotional that had I been in the least bit pessimistic that day, I might have believed Edie when she said she was done with her marriage. But I knew better. Despite their appearing to be on opposite sides of the ring, I sensed that there had to be something Edie and Roy could do differently that would calm them long enough for Roy to get help with his depression and for Edie to diffuse her anger.

We talked at length about what bothered them about their marriage. After they both let off some steam, the hurt beneath their anger emerged. Edie couldn't fathom how Roy could ignore her plea for physical closeness even though he was depressed. He made no effort whatsoever to help her feel secure and wanted. He just kept repeating his mantra, "I'm just not into it." End of story.

Once Roy examined his feelings more thoroughly, he admitted that his disinterest in sex wasn't just about depression. He divulged that whenever he feels pressured into something, he balks; he pulls in the opposite direction. Edie's pushing on this sexual issue made Roy feel that if he were to reach out and touch her, he would be giving in and not be true to himself.

He admitted this wasn't a good way to look at things, but the tug of war went on. A battle for control was claiming their marriage.

I asked Edie, "Even if Roy were to tackle his depression successfully, it wouldn't happen overnight. But what could he do in the meantime that might make you want to stay?" This wasn't easy for her to answer, but eventually she said, "I don't know if he can do this, but he has to show he cares. He has to do something to be close to me sexually. That's all I've been asking for."

And before Roy could protest that he wasn't interested in sex, I asked Edie, "If Roy weren't quite ready to make love, what would be one or two small things he could do that would help you feel closer to him sexually?" The floodgates opened. Edie said, "I need him to hold me. I need him to tell me I'm beautiful and sexy. I need to know that his lack of interest isn't about me. We don't need to have intercourse, but there are things he could do for me, even if he doesn't want to have sex. We used to have oral sex all the time, and I love it. But even if he weren't up for that, if he would just touch me, massage me, I would feel that he cares about my feelings. That might make a difference. I just don't have faith that he'll do it."

I told Edie that I understood her cautiousness. After all, it had been two years since they were physically intimate. Then I said to Roy, "I know you haven't been in the mood for sex, but are you in the mood to save your marriage?" I got a resounding yes. Then I said, "I've got some advice for you. We'll talk about what needs to happen in your life so that you start feeling better inside. That will take some time. But in the meantime, are you willing to show your commitment to saving your marriage by giving Edie more of what she needs, even if you're not feeling turned on yourself? Are you willing to push yourself to be close to her in this way?"

His next yes wasn't quite as resounding because he had something he wanted Edie to do as well. He wanted her to make more of an effort to listen to him when he was feeling down. He wanted her to be a friend, not a drill sergeant. He said, "I will definitely meet Edie halfway, but I need her help. I want my best friend back. I married her because she was kind and had a big heart. I haven't seen those qualities in her for a long time. When I'm down, all I really want her to say is, 'I wish you were feeling better,' or 'I understand how you feel,' not, 'Get over it.' Yes, Michele, I want and am willing to be there for Edie. I will to do what it takes to get things back on track, but I need her too." Edie acknowledged Roy's request and agreed to try harder as well.

Happily, their marriage survived their two-year intimacy famine. I saw them for four months, and Roy was in considerably better spirits by the end. They were making love again, and their friendship that had come precipitously close to dying had clearly been resurrected.

• Don't mind-read.

Don't mind-read, and don't expect your spouse to mind-read. Be clear about what you want and need to have a better sexual relationship. No matter how much you love your spouse or s/he loves you, it won't enable you to be clairvoyant. And by the way, you don't always have to talk to get your point across. You can groan, grunt, moan, and use that hands-on approach.

• Keep your spouse up-to-date.

If you and your spouse have ongoing conversations about sex, that's great. But if your conversations are few and far between, it could present problems because over time, people's sexual preferences and interests can and often do change. What strikes your fancy at one time might not have appeal a few months or years later. It's important to tune into yourself and notice how your body and mind are changing all the time. And when you figure out that something is different, you have to update your spouse. S/he will still be assuming that what you told him or her during your last conversation still stands. Old information leads to boring or unsatisfying sex.

I worked with a woman who, in the early years of her marriage, loved nothing more than when her husband would hold still when they had sex. She loved the feeling of his penis in her engorged vagina. Slight movements felt really sensual to her. But several children later, hormone fluctuations, and a hysterectomy, she found that minimal stimulation wasn't doing the job anymore. Now she likes fast movements. But she failed to share this information with her husband, who, like a good soldier, was just following orders—moving slowly.

It wasn't until I urged them to have an open discussion about her needs that their sexual relationship improved. He was more than happy to oblige. In fact, he preferred more active intercourse himself. It's important to give your spouse information that is hot off the press. Leave the past in the past.

- **Leave the past in the past.**

Sometimes people have trouble feeling desirous toward their spouse if there has been an infidelity. I want you to know a couple of things about infidelity.

First, it is definitely not a marital death sentence. Millions of people not only survive infidelity, they manage to get their marriage back on track and find themselves feeling more loving and connected than ever before. This doesn't happen overnight, and it's not easy by any means. It takes a lot of hard work on both people's parts, but it happens all the time.

Sometimes when people are healing from a betrayal in the past, they have a rough time putting the past in the past, and it dampens desire greatly. If this is one of the primary reasons you've pulled away from your spouse, I understand how you feel. And it's not just a matter of snapping your fingers and pulling yourself out of this emotional mess you're in. Infidelity is devastating to a marriage. Your whole world crashes in on you.

However, you need to do something to move you and your spouse beyond the hurt so that you can restore feelings of intimacy, love, and connection. The fact that you're reading this book speaks volumes about your commitment to making things better. But this book isn't geared toward providing all the help you might need to get things back on track. You have to take additional steps. You can start by reading Chapter 10, "Infidelity," in my last book, *The Divorce Remedy*. It will give you some specific ideas about how to get a grip on your emotions—with your spouse's help, of course. There are many other good books about this topic, and I suggest you read some or, if you're still holding on to the past, get yourself a therapist who can help you work through the pain. As long as you hang on to the past, you will be preventing yourself from feeling close to your spouse.

- **No exaggeration.**

Do you remember those two nasty fighting words, *always* and *never*? They wreak havoc during sex talk too. See for yourself.

"You never initiate sex. I'm always the one to be chasing you."

"You're never romantic before we make love. You just expect me to be in the mood automatically."

"Why do you always want to talk before we have sex? What can't you ever just have a quickie and be done with it?"

By now, you should know what happens when statements or questions such as these are asked. Instead of discussing the issues at hand, couples become defensive and debate how frequently those problem areas actually do occur. But that's not the point, is it?

It's much more helpful to avoid generalizing and exaggerating if you don't want to push your spouse's buttons. Instead of saying, "I'm always the one pursuing you," try saying, "It seems to me that I pursue you more often than you pursue me. I would really like it if you would put out more effort and tell me that you want to make love once in a while." A bit different, isn't it?

And speaking of exaggeration, people often do it without thinking. One of the most puzzling and even humorous things that happens in my office when I talk about sex with couples is how incredibly different their perspectives are about what actually happens in their bedrooms. For example, if I ask, "How frequently do you make love?" I often wonder if the two spouses answering my question are actually in the same marriage because I hear two very different accounts. One spouse will say, "One or two times a week," and the other will, with a look of disbelief, reply, "Excuse me, it's more like one or two times a month!" It's not that people are intentionally under- or overestimating the level of their sexual activity; it's just that their disparate starting points—one person wants very little sex and one person wants lots—color their perceptions. Everything in life, including sex, is relative.

- ### *Don't get discouraged if your partner doesn't follow your lead right away.*

If talking about sex is new to both of you and you're taking the lead, congratulations. I know this has been challenging. But you're doing it for a very good reason. You want a better sexual relationship, and talking frankly about sex is an important step in getting there.

Since this is very new to both of you, your spouse may not be as at ease with talking as you are. When you reveal your thoughts and feelings, your spouse might not be as open as you would like him or her to be. Perhaps, out of embarrassment, s/he starts joking around or evading the conversation. Or maybe s/he has a very difficult time being specific. Whatever the roadblocks to clear communication might be, it's important that you don't get frustrated and clam up. Just take a deep breath, and keep going. With a little practice, you'll both get better at it, and if you don't, you can always get some help from a trained sex therapist.

*   *   *

Talking about your sexual relationship should be something you do regularly. You don't have to have Big Talks all the time, but part of being intimate involves an ongoing sharing of your thoughts about sex. And you don't have to be so serious all the time. I worked with one couple who often used humor to diffuse potentially uncomfortable and conflictual situations. Although I worked with this couple long ago, I will never forget two stories they told me about how they diverted arguments by making each other laugh.

They were having their two millionth discussion about their different sexual appetites. Ken was complaining that Lisa wasn't interested enough. Lisa, defending herself, said, "Ken, I don't think you're being completely honest when you blame me for our infrequent sex. Actually, the truth is, if you think about it, there are really only two times when I'm not into it." And before she could elaborate, Ken interjected, "Yeah, whenever I want to and every other time." After a second of silence, Lisa cracked up. Ken joined her. They had a great day together and great sex that night.

Another time, Lisa was, as usual, in the midst of defending herself, "You know, Ken, I talk to other couples, and we could be having a lot less sex than we do," to which Ken responded, "Lisa, that would be impossible. We'd be getting into anti-matter." Again, they laughed.

Yes, sex is serious business, but lighten up folks. Annie Hall said, "Sex is the most fun I've ever had without laughing."

And now, my parting thoughts.

CHAPTER TEN

Afterglow

Now that you've read all of the marriage-enriching, desire-boosting methods and stories about people who have rediscovered the passion in their lives, I'm going to come clean. You and your spouse may never, ever bridge your desire gap. You may both, throughout the rest of your married lives, still feel exactly the same way about sex that you do right now. In fact, research tells us that 69 percent of what couples in healthy marriages argue about is resolvable (Gottman and Silver, 1999)! Researchers eavesdropped on newlywed couples to hear their heated issues. Years later, they eavesdropped again and head exactly the same stuff! So, the truth is, you and your spouse may always have different sexual appetites.

But before you start wondering why I would end my book on a pessimistic note, you should know me better by now. I wouldn't do that. I have one more word of inspiration and encouragement to share with you before we part. I want to tell you something personal about me.

In the early years of my marriage, my husband, Jim, and I could have been one of the couples about whom I have written. We were truly on different planets in regard to our sexual desires. I thought he was insatiable and he thought my sexual well had run dry. There were more arguments, tears, and days of silence than I care to admit. But we both stood our ground. After all, I had to. I was the "relationship expert." I knew that our sex life, though unsatisfying to Jim, was well within normal bounds. And I spent too many years trying to prove it to him rather than listening to his feelings. Jim didn't make my wanting him any easier in those days. His anger and frustration made him, well, let's just say, he wasn't the nicest person to be around. (Sorry, Jim.)

But thankfully, I'm really blessed by my work. Thousands of couples trust me enough to invite me into the complex, fascinating, challenging, and often poignant stories of their lives. They share their innermost thoughts and feelings. I feel privileged to share such intimate moments with them. It is from them that I have learned a great deal about life, love, and intimacy. My more highly sexed clients taught me what goes on in the hearts and minds of people when their life partners say no. I learned it's not just about sex. And when I incorporated what I learned into my relationship with Jim, it changed our lives together.

I decided that I loved Jim so much, I wanted him to feel wanted. I didn't want there to be a separation between us anymore because of sexual differences. I vowed to myself that I would do whatever I had to do to refocus my energies and make sexuality a more significant priority in our lives— not just for Jim, but for us.

Does this mean that we have sex all the time, several times a day? Absolutely not. But before I tell you what has happened, I must digress a moment to tell you an interesting story. Although I am quite petite, when I was a little girl, I was fat. People used to tease me all the time. I weigh less now than I did when I was eleven years old. I'm small. As a young adult who had gotten her weight under control, I looked back at my chubby past and found myself blaming my mother for not having forced better eating habits on me. I also promised myself that when I had children of my own, I would approach parenting differently. And so, when our two children were growing up, my shopping list never included cookies, ice cream and chocolates, or anything else children love. My kids were the ones eating raisins and carrots sticks, the ones whose Easter baskets were filled with fat-free licorice, jelly beans, and nonedible delights.

It should have been no surprise to me that every chance my kids got— birthday parties, field trips, visits to relatives' houses—they would gorge themselves on what they couldn't have at home. They couldn't get enough. As they got older, it became more and more of a struggle to keep them in line. Eating yummy foods had almost become a preoccupation, and they had the waistlines to show for it.

Eventually I decided to stop being the junk food gestapo. I bit my tongue when they went for their second helping of ice cream. I even started bringing home cookies and other goodies. Their Easter baskets had chocolate eggs and chocolate bunnies. At first, there was a veritable feeding frenzy, and this lasted for a while. But then, slowly yet perceptibly, things changed. The forbidden fruit lost its appeal. They could take or leave the bag of potato chips with their lunches. And now, licorice and gummy bears—fat-free candy—are what I see them grab as they rush out the door. Life is funny, isn't it?

What does this story have to do with Jim and me? Once Jim recognized that I truly understood his hurt, his sense of rejection, and his desire to be close to me sexually, and once he saw that I was devoted to bringing back the passion in our lives, something within him changed. Like all other couples, our lives are hectic, and there are lots of times when we get sexually out of sync. But now, rather than feel hurt, rejected, or angry, he knows that just happens sometimes. Plus, he feels confident that if he "needs" me, I'm never too far away. That's important to me.

The rewards I've received for loving him in this way have been immeasurable. He's been a happy man. After nearly three decades together, our marriage has never been stronger. We are like two giddy newlyweds, and we've been this way for so long. We talk, we laugh, we share, we make love. Bridging the desire gap isn't about having more or less sex; it's about loving each other.

I tell you this because I can easily recall those dark times early on when our sexual differences divided us. I'm certain you've had dark times of your own. But I want you to know that no matter how distant you and your spouse may feel, it's never too late to have a loving, intimate, mutually satisfying sexual relationship. *Never.* It's never too late to rediscover the pleasures of sex and the bond that comes from being in sync sexually.

Although endings are always bittersweet for me, especially because I never feel done, I know one person who will be happy it's over: Jim. I think I'll give him a call and ask if he wants to fool around.

Selected Bibliography

Basson, R. "Using a Different Model for Female Sexual Response to Address Women's Problematic Low Sexual Desire." *Journal of Sex and Marital Therapy* 27 (2001): 395–403.

Berman, J. R., L. A. Berman, and E. Bumiller. *For Women Only: A Revolutionary Guide to Overcoming Sexual Dysfunction and Reclaiming Your Sex Life.* New York: Holt, 2001.

Crenshaw, T. L. *The Alchemy of Love and Lust.* New York: Putnam, 1996.

Gochros, H. L., and J. Fischer. *Treat Yourself to a Better Sex Life.* Upper Saddle River, N.J.: Prentice Hall, 1980.

Gottman, J. M., and N. Silver. *The Seven Principles for Making Marriage Work.* New York: Crown, 1999.

Kaplan, H. S. "Hypoactive Sexual Desire." *Journal of Sex and Marital Therapy* 3 (1979): 3–9.

Laumann, E., A. Paik, and R. Rosen. "Sexual Dysfunction in the United States: Prevalence, Predictors, and Outcomes." *Journal of the American Medical Association* 10 (1999): 537.

Love, P. *The Truth About Love.* New York: Fireside Books, 2001.

Love, P., and J. Robinson. *Hot Monogamy.* New York: Penguin Books, 1994.

Markman, H. J., S. M. Stanley, and S. L. Blumberg. *Fighting for Your Marriage.* San Francisco: Jossey-Bass, 2001.

Masters, W. H., and V. E. Johnson. *Human Sexual Response.* Boston: Little, Brown, 1966.

Prochaska, J. O., J. C. Norcross, and C. C. DiClemente. *Changing for Good.* New York: Avon Books, 1994.

Schnarch, D. *Passionate Marriage.* New York: Holt, 1997.

Weiner Davis, M. *Change Your Life and Everyone in It.* New York: Simon & Schuster, 1996.

Weiner Davis, M. *The Divorce Remedy.* New York: Simon & Schuster, 2001.

Recommended Reading

Barbach, L. *For Each Other: Sharing Sexual Intimacy.* New York: Signet, 2001.

Berman, J. R., L. A. Berman, and E. Bumiller. *For Women Only: A Revolutionary Guide to Overcoming Sexual Dysfunction and Reclaiming Your Sex Life.* New York: Holt, 2001.

Castleman, J. *The Playbook for Men About Sex.* San Francisco: Down There Press, 1981.

Comfort, Alex. *The Joy of Sex.* New York: Crown, 1972.

———. *The New Joy of Sex.* New York: Crown, 1991.

Crenshaw, T. L. *The Alchemy of Love and Lust: Discovering Our Sex Hormones and How They Determine Who We Love, When We Love, and How Often We Love.* New York: Putnam, 1996.

Gochros, H. L., and J. Fischer. *Treat Yourself to a Better Sex Life.* Upper Saddle River, N.J.: Prentice Hall, 1980.

Gottman, J. M., and N. Silver. *The Seven Principles for Making Marriage Work.* New York: Crown, 1999.

Love, P. *The Truth About Love: The Highs, the Lows and How You Can Make It Last Forever.* New York: Fireside Books, 2001.

Love, P., and J. Robinson. *Hot Monogamy: Essential Steps to More Passionate, Intimate Lovemaking.* New York: Penguin Books, 1994.

Markman, H. J., S. M. Stanley, and S. L. Blumberg. *Fighting for Your Marriage: Positive Steps for Preventing Divorce and Preserving a Lasting Love.* San Francisco: Jossey-Bass, 2001.

Reichman, J. *I'm Not in the Mood: What Every Woman Should Know About Improving Her Libido.* New York: Morrow, 1998.

Schnarch, D. *Passionate Marriage: Keeping Love and Intimacy Alive in Committed Relationships.* New York: Holt, 1997.

Weiner Davis, M. *Change Your Life and Everyone in It.* New York: Simon & Schuster, 1996.

Weiner Davis, M. *The Divorce Remedy.* New York: Simon & Schuster, 2001.

Zilbergeld, Bernie. *The New Male Sexuality: The Truth About Men, Sex, and Pleasure.* New York: Bantam, 1992.

Index

Michele Weiner Davis is the author of *The Divorce Remedy, Divorce Busting, A Woman's Guide to Changing Her Man, Change Your Life and Everyone in It,* and *In Search of Solutions.* A regular guest on *Oprah* and an internationally renowned seminar leader and marriage therapist in private practice, she lives with her family in Illinois.

You can visit Michele at www.divorcebusting.com.